STEPLADDER TO HINDSIGHT

Also by Richard Freadman

Eliot, James and the Fictional Self: A Study in Character and Narration (1986)

On Literary Theory and Philosophy: A Cross-Disciplinary Encounter (ed. with Lloyd Reinhardt) (1991)

Re-thinking Theory: A Critique of Contemporary Literary Theory and an Alternative Account (co-authored with Seumas Miller) (1992)

Renegotiating Ethics in Literature, Theory, Philosophy (ed. with Jane Adamson and David Parker) (1998)

Threads of Life: Autobiography and the Will (2001)

Shadow of Doubt: My Father and Myself (2003)

This Crazy Thing a Life: Australian Jewish Autobiography (2007)

Jovial Harbinger of Doom: Short Stories of Laurie Clancy (ed.) (2014)

Stepladder to Hindsight
An Almost Memoir

Richard Freadman

HYBRID
PUBLISHERS

Published by Hybrid Publishers

Melbourne Victoria Australia

© Richard Freadman 2016

This publication is copyright. Apart from any use
as permitted under the Copyright Act 1968, no part may be
reproduced by any process without prior written permission
from the publisher. Requests and enquiries concerning
reproduction should be addressed to the Publisher,
Hybrid Publishers,
PO Box 52, Ormond, VIC Australia 3204.

www.hybridpublishers.com.au

First published 2016

Creator: Freadman, Richard, 1951– author.
Title: Stepladder to hindsight / Richard Freadman.
ISBN: 9781925272192 (paperback)
      9781925280487 (ebook)
Subjects: Freadman, Richard, 1951–
          Self-actualization (Psychology) in middle age.
          Men—Identity.

Dewey Number: 920.71

Cover design: Art on Order
Typeset in Adobe Garamond Pro 11.5/15.3

Cover image: ©Yastremska/Bigstock.com

In memoriam

Rosalie Fleur Freadman

30 December 1928—4 December 2012

Contents

Preface

This is a book about a man who reaches a turning point in his life and looks back. The turning point is retirement and since that man is me, it is, in a sense, an autobiography. The sort of looking back I do is partly a matter of age. But it is also, of course, a reflection of who I am. And like all of us, "I" am not one thing but many: a many-faceted being. Sometimes I look back in the manner of a retired academic and writer, sometimes as one who has been a family man for over thirty years, with many of the complexities that can involve. Elsewhere I write as an ordinary guy who loves sport, friendship, animals, and has often found life infinitely strange, funny and, at times, incredibly sad. Life has always seemed to me to go very deep and I hope this comes through in these pages. As you'd expect, my various facets and voices sometimes intertwine.

This is not the story of a famous life: though well educated and reasonably successful, I have done nothing special. But any life is potentially significant and interesting if its textures, moods, themes, turning points, disappointments, and the people of importance to it are described with nuance, feeling, and honesty.

The reader who is expecting a continuous chronological narrative from birth to the time of writing will be disappointed. This looking back involves only a loose chronological sequence. The book is written in a genre that is sometimes called "discontinuous narrative." It focuses on moments, phases, and people in my life, all of them connected by the themes that unfold throughout: what it means to age; the rewards, disappointments, and deceptions of a life driven by a career; family; friendship; our relationships with animals; and, in very general terms, what it means to flourish as a human being—to realize the best of one's potential in a particular time and place.

When we write about others at length in our own life stories we inevitably move beyond autobiography. To focus a narrative on someone else is to write biography. *Stepladder to Hindsight* is hybrid writing of myself and others. It could be called auto/biography, memoir or almost-memoir: a narrative about other people seen from the vantage point of one who shared something of life with them. Sometimes this sharing takes the form of long friendships, at others, chance one-off encounters which stay in the mind for their strangeness, their curious quality of fleeting momentousness.

The book contains a thread of reflection on the narrative structures of lives and the narrative forms we use to write about those lives. This reflects my longstanding interest in the field of "life writing."

The chapters in the book can be read as freestanding pieces or as part of the loose sequence in which they sit. For those dipping in, a list of key characters follows. Chapters can be read out of order or in order. If I get too academic for you in places, skip a few paragraphs, pages or a chapter.

Richard Freadman
Melbourne and Florida, 2016

Thank you

Many people, including family, friends, literary colleagues, and those who have provided advice on some of my medical themes, have contributed to the writing of this book. My thanks to Roger Averill, Doris Brett, Carol Burton, John Cocks, Dianne Clifton, Tom Couser, Colin Davidson, Stephen Davis, David Derby, John Eakin, John Gatt-Rutter, the late Hugh Kiernan, the late David Parker, Mark Maimone, Jeff Maimone, Miriam Mills, Wendy Prellwitz, Alan Shapiro, Rick Shapiro, Penny Wayne, Ron Shapiro, Kate Shepherd, Arnold Zable and Barbara Zabel.

Special thanks as always to my family, Diane, Ben, Maddie and Elliot.

Sincere thanks too to Hybrid Publishers, who have been a delight to work with. My talented editor, Ali Arnold, has made this a better book than it would otherwise have been. Had I actioned more of her suggestions it would no doubt be better still.

Key people in the book

Fleur Freadman (my mother)

Paul Freadman (my father)

Diane Shelton (my wife: academic and business person)

Elliot "Elli" Shelton Freadman (our son)

Madeleine "Maddie" Shelton Freadman (our daughter)

Ben Meiklejohn (my stepson)

Peanut Freadman (our cat)

Haggis Freadman (schnoodle), and McDuff Freadman (Australian wirehair terrier)

Renata Maimone (my mentor and friend)

Jeff Maimone (elder son of Renata and Joe Maimone)

Mark Maimone (younger son and old friend)

Margaretha Maimone (musician and spouse of Mark)

Rick Shapiro (old friend, businessman and Shakespeare scholar)

Penny Wayne (musician and spouse of Rick)

Ben Shapiro (son of Penny and Rick)

Joan Wayne (mother of Penny)

Ron Barassi (my childhood football hero)

Allen Grossman (Professor of English at Brandeis University)

Ian Guthridge (high school teacher)

One

Stepladder to hindsight, or, the careerist retires

[Mr. Casaubon's] soul was sensitive without being enthusiastic: it was too languid to thrill out of self-consciousness into passionate delight; it went on fluttering in the swampy ground where it was hatched, thinking of its wings and never flying.

—George Eliot, *Middlemarch*

They cannot scare me with their empty spaces
Between stars—on stars where no human race is.
I have it in me so much nearer home
To scare myself with my own desert places.

—Robert Frost, "Desert Places"

"Gentlemen, start your engines—and may the best woman win!"

—Ru Paul, *RuPaul's Drag Race*

⸺

Retirement! I was packing up and vacating my book-lined office and had just come to the most battered book of all among the five hundred or so on the wall behind my desk. *Middlemarch* by George Eliot, published in 1873, had commanded my attention in the mid- to late-1970s more than any other book before or since. Perhaps a dozen fiercely attentive readings over that period, and one a couple of years earlier, had smashed the binding of the gray and white paperback Riverside edition. It was now secured by a thick rubber band around its 600-page girth. A small bulldog clip clasped fifteen index cards to the grubby, fading front cover, which announced that this edition had been edited by the doyen of George Eliot scholarship, Gordon S. Haight, of Yale University, a man whose name consorted curiously with Eliot's impassioned commendations of the power of love. I had, like an exegete at Holy Scripture, painstakingly filled the index cards with quotes, lists of themes and page numbers from the great novel, each card prefaced by a topic heading in red biro: "Jealousy, fear, love"; "Language and perspective"; "Feeling and intellect"; "Egoism"; "Narration"; "Men and women"; "Self-knowledge and the knowledge of others"; "Sympathy," and so on.

Cradling the ragged book in one hand, I edged down my little aluminum stepladder, sat in my desk chair, and wondered what all *that* had been about.

My sixth-floor office was lovely and spacious, with sweeping views on two sides of gum trees, a moat, and the far corners of the La Trobe University campus—a campus built on farm land in the 1960s. From this vantage point of age and experience, the cards, like the heavily penciled grids of underlining and annotation on many of the book's pages, were sharp reminders of the clenched will that drove that young PhD candidate—his search for whatever it was he thought he was after, in a booth-like wooden desk in the Upper Reading Room of Oxford's 400-year-old, castle-like Gothic Bodleian Library. Now, to my 64-year-old self, the vast effort of that youthful aspirant—"the long spasm of his too-fixed attention," as Henry James wonderfully said of fellow novelist Flaubert—looked a touch misguided, obsessive even, almost quaint. Yet, this older self was so much the product of that feverishly ambitious, anxious, muddled earlier one. Without intense immersion in that life-changing book, and without the compulsions that fuelled it, I would not have been there, reviewing the professional life that was coming to an end.

When I first read *Middlemarch* as an undergraduate in America, I was conducting a long-distance relationship with a girl in Virginia, and was knocked sideways by sexual jealousy and suspicion—a torment so overwhelming that I felt at times it could bring me undone. There was also a thread of sexual jealousy in *Middlemarch*: the desiccated old pedant, cleric-scholar Edward Casaubon, rightly suspecting that his ardent young wife, Dorothea, was attracted to his vibrant young cousin, the ominously named Will Ladislaw. But the novel's greatest fascination for me lay not in Casaubon's sexual jealousy but in its exploration of the deeper sources of such jealousy—in him and in others, including me. *Why* did it have such a consuming, pathological grip on me?

Middlemarch sees Casaubon as a brooding conflu-
ence of many kinds of casualty. He's a casualty of what
the narrator, with her genius for haunting philosophical
reflection, calls "the terrible stringency of human need."
The human being just tends to be a tremendously needy
creature. I certainly was and have always been so. But why
was Casaubon so unable to make a measure of peace with
that need, and why was I making such an incontinent hash
of my situation?

Middlemarch calls Casaubon's inner emotional and
moral state "egoism." Nowadays we'd probably call it
narcissism: that deceiving condition which often looks like
"self-love" but actually has its sources in deep, often unconscious, feelings of inner deficit that may date from earliest
infancy. George Eliot reckons that we are all born egoists,
"taking the world as an udder to feed our supreme selves,"
but that those who make viable transitions into adulthood
emerge, though not entirely, from egoism into a moral and
psychological condition she associates with the capacity
for "sympathy," open and empathic communication with
others. Casaubon hadn't done that. He was dogged and
stultified by his own nagging, narcissistic self-doubt—a
point the novel makes through penetrating psychological
analysis and brilliant metaphors and images that accompany the poor man all the way to the grave and, indeed,
beyond: dried-up rivulets, enclosed basins, labyrinths,
mazes, his soul as a bird hatched in a swamp and unable to
take flight, his emotional legacy a dead hand.

His self-fashioned maze found its perfect medium of

expression in the index card. The poor man thought – or nervously hoped—that he'd discovered "the key to all mythologies," and he had myths indexed and cross-referenced to within an inch of their lives. Did it ever occur to me that when I entered references to Casaubon on my own sheath of index cards I was in effect Casaubonizing Casaubon? Or was such a colossal irony lost on my younger self? I don't know. From the vantage point of retirement, I'd be inclined to say that I was too driven and uncertain back then to reflect on this, or indeed on much else, to very good effect. I knew very little about how to live. But then again, how much do I know—I mean *really* know—about how to live, forty years later?

Middlemarch doesn't condemn the unfortunate Casaubon, and neither does it pretend that knowing how to live is easy. Another of those luminous philosophical reflections speaks of our need for self-protective emotional systems and filters in response to a world which would be too much for anyone to cope with unarmored: "If we had a keen vision and feeling of all ordinary human life, it would be like hearing the grass grow and the squirrel's heartbeat, and we should die of that roar which lies on the other side of silence." So everyone needs to be what Eliot calls "well wadded with stupidity": a bit blind, a bit self-deceived, a bit selective in what we allow ourselves to see and acknowledge about ourselves.

I keenly identified with Casaubon's insecurity as a scholar. Later I was to realize that most people have an activity or a moral ideal that they use as a yardstick for assessing their overall personal worth. Fail *there* and it feels as though you've failed completely. My activity at that time was scholarship. Having put all of my ego eggs, so to speak, in that basket, I'd made the PhD—a testing process for even the most robust of souls—a sort of make-or-break obstacle race. Casaubon's narcissistic over-investment in scholarship and its silent accomplice, self-doubt, had upped the ante for him too and had rendered him preternaturally sensitive to professional criticism. Deep down, below the surface of conscious awareness, he wondered whether the "key" was real, whether he might not, in fact, have wasted decades of his life.

And what about the girl in Virginia? Well, it turned out that my suspicions were well founded: she had in fact got involved with someone else. But so, come to think of it, had I—though only, I told myself, because I knew what she was up to.

———— ∞ ————

So now, with almost nauseating suddenness, the professional life through which I'd sought identity and validation was basically over, give or take the odd lecture, article, book, review or commendation in someone else's footnote. In *Being Mortal*, Atul Gawande's enlightened study of how contemporary Western society negotiates—and often avoids dealing with—old age, he argues that the "radical concept of retirement" started to take shape in the industrial era. It's perhaps more accurate to say that economic forces made retirement more widely available than it had been hitherto, because the aristocratic classes had long been able to retire, to *step back* as the French *retirer* translates, from civic or military life into a state of blessed seclusion.

One such was the Renaissance humanist Michel de Montaigne, pioneer of the autobiographical essay and a forerunner of modern speculative consciousness. In his *Essays*, this writer, whom his younger contemporary, Shakespeare, may have read later in life, refers to himself as the "I, who watch myself as narrowly as I can, and who have my eyes continually bent upon myself." Yet Montaigne was also a worldly man of high civic accomplishment and reputation. When he withdrew from public life into the seclusion of a tower in the family chateau in 1571, he immersed himself in a library of 1500 books that covered, like his *Essays*, a vast range of topics. After ten years of wonderfully creative seclusion, Montaigne re-entered public life to become Mayor of Bordeaux, as his father had been, but in 1571 he had welcomed retirement with open arms:

> Since God gives us leisure to order our removal, let us make ready, truss our baggage, take leave betimes of the company, and disentangle ourselves from those violent importunities that engage us elsewhere and separate us from ourselves.

These "importunities" included the French religious wars that raged on for the last thirty years of his life (he died in 1592) and beyond. Though Montaigne seems to have been as "well wadded" against such strife as any profoundly reflective person can be, he believed with Socrates that "the unexamined life is not worth living." Above all, the "examined" life allows us to prepare for dying, "which is the greatest work we have to do." To cultivate what he calls the "contempt of death" is to achieve philosophical and spiritual calm in the face of approaching mortality. The preparation for death, I now see, is a form of retirement work.

It's remarkable how clearly Montaigne foresaw the dangers, so familiar to us now, of a split between the public self, which seeks validation and approbation through visible achievement, and the private, authentic self—that deeper, more personal sense of "who I really am" that Western modernity has since adopted as its gold standard of human flourishing. The quest for this authentic self was to become far more anguished in the hands of Rousseau, transformative genius of French eighteenth-century autobiography. But clearly Montaigne had good protection against inner division. "I have not the knack of nourishing quarrels and debates in my own bosom." He was no Hamlet and, quite unlike Rousseau, he seems to have been generally comfortable in his own skin.

How I admire, even envy, this man's existential self-sufficiency! Unlike Casaubon, he does not crave the approval of others. "I do not value myself on any other account than because I know my own value," he writes. Robust self-esteem—what Proust calls "self-sufficient well-being"—seems to come naturally to him, as a sort of gift of upbringing and temperament. But this is too simple: Montaigne clearly had to sustain, maybe even recreate, his self by writing it. His modernity lies partly in his sense that the self is a thing-in-process, not a monument or a destination. He says of writing himself, "I do not paint its being, I paint its passage."

—

I've often thought there are four great human demographics: those who are born confident, those who achieve confidence, those for whom confidence comes and goes depending on mood and circumstance, and those who never know the feeling. The son of under-confident parents, I'm of the third dispensation. And so, when I look directly across my office at the narrow bookcase squat enough to nestle under the windowsill, I feel like a man gazing at a somewhat amateur extension he's built by hand to the family home. This is the bookcase that houses copies of the books and articles I've written over four decades. Certainly, the extension gets the job done—a rumpus room for growing kids, a much-needed guest room—but the kids will have to wedge folded paper under the legs of the pool table if the snooker balls aren't going to follow the contours of the rumpus room's sloping floor. The skills on show don't tally with my exorbitant ambition, and there's been collateral damage from all that drive and striving—the self-centeredness, the obsession, the fatigue, the angst at real or perceived failures. The narrator of *Middlemarch* observes of Dorothea: "She was always trying to be what her husband wished, and never able to repose on his delight in what she was." This reflection on the gender politics of a traditional marriage applies more generally to the damage done by chronic self-absorption.

My daughter, Madeleine, already in receipt of many of the philosophy books from my office, has unhappy childhood memories of feeling unwelcome at the threshold of my study door. And when my wife, Diane, a voracious reader who prefers not to be written about, came to the place in Henry James' novel *The Golden Bowl* where the character Adam Verver is described as "a man who could be interrupted with impunity," she was quick to remind me that I am no Adam Verver. The sense of "emotional intermittence" my family bemoans in me is part of the collateral damage wrought by people who over-invest in their professional lives, hoping to assuage what Robert Frost calls the "desert places" within. The title *Middlemarch* indicates the middle-of-the-road path on which most self-absorbed strivers will eventually find themselves, including those like me, who meant to "alter the world a little."

Maddie, at twenty-three, was lying full length on the living room sofa, a hideous lilac toweling dressing gown draped over her Simpsons pajamas, and two dogs and a laptop draped over her. Elbows above dog level, she was working at an intricate piece of needlework; her eyes, when not fixed on the needle, flitted to some of the least appealing television I could imagine. Two drained coffee cups sat on the glass table beside a copy of Sartre's *Being and Nothingness*, one of the texts for her Honors degree in Philosophy. Two rooms away, in the kitchen, I was making a coffee when she called out over the cacophony of the TV something about Sartre's notion of "bad faith."

"*What?*" I called back. "I can't hear over that racket."

"Well, come here then. I shouldn't have to *shout!*"

So I made my way into her space, a dog tail wagging the laptop as she paused Foxtel and said: "There seem to be different versions of bad faith. Sartre's waiter"—in *Being and Nothingness*—"tries to disappear into the role of waiter 'cause he doesn't want the burden of having a free self; the girl on the date who lets her arm become dead meat when the guy she's with goes to hold her hand is refusing to choose. It's like it becomes a phantom arm with no connection to her."

This was a new insight to me and I was immediately engrossed—we share a love of ideas. We chatted on about how each of the people in Sartre's example wants personal identity delivered to them on a platter without any of the angst of fashioning an identity for themselves. That's the way they've been trained to live. But each will feel, perhaps without ever knowing it, the angst of inauthenticity, of not being true to the self, of not fashioning a dynamic self to which they can be true.

The pause button was released and the cacophony resumed. I turned to the TV to see its source. It looked at first as though a bunch of superannuated amateur opera singers loaded with champagne and dodgy pharmaceuticals were mincing about in a state of hysteria.

"What the fuck is *that?*" I inquired. "Who *are* these people? Poor bloody women!"

"They're men," Maddie replied matter-of-factly. "Drag queens. It's *RuPaul's Drag Race.*"

I'd heard the kids chatting about a televised drag race and had wondered why they'd be interested in petrol-headed pursuits. But, no, this was a very different sort of drag racing—a gloriously histrionic version of reality TV in which drag queens, who appear both in and out of role, compete to become America's next leading monarch of the catwalk, among other things. With due philosophical rigor the criteria for success are clearly spelled out—acronyms optional—for contestants, judging panel and viewers: Charisma, Uniqueness, Nerve and Talent.

The play on "drag queen" is announced in the program logo, where RuPaul, the high camp Aerial of the piece, appears clad in a lady's pink lycra bodysuit and holding two chequered flags. In each episode "she" launches the contestants into their challenge with the exhortation: "Gentlemen, start your motors and may the best woman win!"

The contests in this particular program involved be-ing photographed fully clothed in a tank of water, and constructing "couture" out of materials—everything from curtains to colored plastic sheeting—plundered from dumpsters in Hollywood. Great care went into making the garments for the fashion contest to come. But perhaps the greatest care had gone into the contestants' fashion-ing of their queenly persona names: I was rather hoping that Penny Tration would win, simply on account of her name's elegant simplicity, though Detox Icunt, and Jinkx Monsoon had also distinguished themselves in the naming game. In the end Jinkx prevailed in a flowing "aquamarine

Grecian" number—another feather in the cap of the self-titled "Seattle's premier Jewish narcoleptic drag queen."

"So, Madeleine," I asked, by now quite curious, "*what* do you see in this? The philosopher among drag queens. Talk about high and low culture!"

"What about *you*, Dad?! The professor of English who spends half his time watching sport and listening to sports talkback radio. You're always on about 'the theatre of football.' What's the difference?"

She had a point. And, come to think of it, when I was Maddie's age I spent hours with Monty Python and frittered away vast tracts of valuable PhD time in the Hertford College Common Room watching cricket of extremely variable quality. I needed wacky diversions, among other props, to help me through the crippling depression that dogged me for many years and surfaced with particular ferocity when I was struggling with my PhD. Yes, she was right. Same pattern, different diversions.

And I was enjoying the high/low culture discussion—probably, at this point, a good deal more than she was.

"But sport is the culture writ large," I said. "It's about how to live and in that sense it's philosophical."

"So is RuPaul. These guys aren't just exhibitionists. The show's about identity. About how to create an identity for yourself if the one you've been given doesn't fit. It's about personhood."

"But aren't these guys just running from male stereotypes to extreme female ones?"

"Yes, but do you think they don't know that? They're

sending up gender roles in general and the drag queen is a sort of gender-mix that breaks all the rules. Did you hear one of them mention performativity?"

I had noticed one of them using the term. I knew it from my academic life and assumed it to be just that—an academic term. But clearly the idea that you create your identity by enacting speculative, invented and desired versions of the self had filtered down to the world of RuPaul. I've always liked it when the academy meets the wider community. It's what university life should be about.

"Performativity's a bit existential, don't you think?" continued Madeleine. "You know, plunging into the unknown to find out what your authentic self might be like, or might feel like."

"QED!" I conceded. "The existential drag race!"

I love her way with ideas, her cultural range. Indeed, as she says, we have these things in common. And I guess it gives her some sense of predictability with her intermittent Old Man to know that a philosophical question will almost always claim his attention. But there's sadness here too. Life can be a battle for her. Her own interior world is rendered unpredictable by the fluctuations of bipolar depression. She needs the theatre and entertainment of kitsch just as I need sport, and her condition looks like a more intense form of the huge ups and downs I suffered at her age. I think it's come down through my family, along with the love of ideas. Genetic legacies are a crapshoot. Maddie's is nothing if not a mixed bag.

She's very open about her condition, which is quite well

controlled now and on the improve, and she has written about it for the benefit of other sufferers and their families. Her main symptom is a frightening thing called "mixed states." In her words:

> The description of the emotional sensation of a mixed episode is elusive. You have the extreme, vicious negativity of the depressive episodes combined with the racing thoughts of a manic episode and, to top it all off, my particular response of shutting down results in a state in which my mind is racing so hard I feel dizzy. I know what I'm hearing and feeling is telling me that I'm the worst, that I'm hopeless, that there's no point in continuing to try and fight it, but it's as if all of this is happening behind the kind of screen you'd see in Indonesian puppet shows. The outline of the feelings are there, but the detail is lost, making it impossible to properly identify the emotions and feelings. It'd be like being at the grand prix, hearing the cars, but seeing an empty race track.

She wrote this at about the same age I was when slogging away at those *Middlemarch* index cards in the Bodleian, and veering in and out of severe depression. The piece in which this paragraph appears is one of the hardest things I've ever had to read and I am haunted by the grand prix metaphor. I felt sure after reading it that, at least with her, my old intermittence would be at an end. But it hasn't been. Old habits die hard. Long-embedded psychological defenses die harder.

In a corner of the office with panoramic views in all directions stood my two half-size gray filing cabinets. The one on the right housed lectures, tutorial notes and other teaching materials. I'd been a fine teacher and very devoted to my students. No self-doubt there. It also contained documents that recalled the history of the La Trobe University Unit for Studies in Biography and Autobiography, of which I'd been the founding director. Never the funding magnet that modern universities demand, it had been the most enjoyable thing I did as an academic: seminars, conferences, visits from people who loved life writing—biography, autobiography, memoir, anything narrative that concerns itself with the contours and meanings of individual lives and lives in-relation with others. I'd been very lucky to have had a passion right at the center of my professional life. And since writing such narratives requires a reflective "stepping back" from the fray, I had a bridge to retirement that others—a surgeon, say, who lays down his scalpel for the last time—may not have.

The filing cabinet to the left was a more mixed affair. In the testimonials I'd written for students and colleagues I saw the best part of my professional self: caring, supportive, nurturing, loyal (when treated loyally). But there was a mountain of other stuff that read—to the extent that I could stand to sample it—as one might feel sipping yesterday's bath water:

> Dear Professor X,
>
> I write to apply for the Senior Lecturer position (XYZ) in your Department of English.

Notwithstanding that the position requires specialist knowledge of German literature, and that I do not know German, as required by the advertisement (my degrees are in English and American literature), I submit this application with real enthusiasm and in the hope that the selection committee might entertain the possibility of a slightly unorthodox appointment (unorthodox in terms of academic specialty, I mean—not with respect to academic promise or accomplishment, in which areas I count myself quite clearly competitive).

It will be assumed—and rightly—that I have read my share of German literature in translation; and, indeed, I have strong interests in German fiction and autobiography that could, quite readily I believe, translate (so to speak!) into productive areas of teaching and publication. I believe that my deep familiarity with autobiography and fiction in English would provide apposite grounds for comparative—English and German—teaching and scholarship.

I believe, too, that my knowledge of German social theory could usefully diversify the Department's theoretical offerings, which are, as I see it, largely focused on French literary and cultural theory. (I do not, needless to say, wish to pronounce on the Department's present curricular arrangements, other than to say that my careful perusal of your handbook entries is one of several factors that have disposed me to lodge the current application with such enthusiasm.)

I believe that my referees would be pleased to speak

to the above remarks and to my publication record which, while not prolific, is I think commendable under the circumstances, and gathering momentum. The enclosed teaching surveys will, I believe, like my CV, demonstrate that I am ready to "hit the ground running," should I be given the opportunity to join your Department.

Please be advised that some of the referee reports you receive may be generic in nature: that is, they will have been crafted for the perusal of various selection committees in their deliberations with respect to various academic positions. This "generic" character, as I have called it, reflects the heavy commitments of eminent figures in our field who have unhesitatingly expressed their willingness to write on my behalf, and should in no way be construed as indicating a pattern of undiscriminating application for jobs on my part. Indeed, as I have said, I find the position you have advertised particularly appealing, notwithstanding my non-specialist engagement with German literature thus far, and would greatly appreciate the opportunity to develop the above thoughts in more detail at an interview, should the selection committee see fit to include me in the short—or even the long-short!—list for this position.

May I say in closing that I have long intended to learn German and would be more than happy to spend the upcoming summer vacation in Germany, learning the language "on the ground," so to speak, with intensive augmentation from a language program at a reputable institution of higher learning, in preparation for the welcome challenges that your position would afford.

My thanks to yourself and the committee for considering the above crock of shit.

Insincerely, and with abject and self-immolating moral turpitude,

Yours,

Uriah Pulltheotherleg Freadman

PS, Please find enclosed an informal letter of commendation from my grandmother, herself (albeit briefly) an academic.

The relief of those paper-recycling bins! File upon file of this stuff filled three jumbo-sized bins, each wad having to be fed through a shark-toothed slit because the bins were locked for secure transport to the shredder downstairs. The amount of crap that one pens in the course of a career! The number of meetings one attends to formulate policy soon to be overturned by the next restructure. Those moral corners cut with all the delicacy of a neurosurgeon, the fibs by omission, and—most irksome of all—that manufactured professional *voice*, tinny as a Caribbean percussion band, but without an atom of its earthy authenticity.

Message to the shredder: Don't just shred the documents. For god's sake, shred that version of the man who wrote them, that he may rise again from the paper fettuccini of his decimation a better man!

Packing up the office had its reflective moments but it was also hard slog and dragged on for weeks, this endless lowering and stacking of books into boxes, taping lids closed, tossing out desk detritus—dead erasers, parched biros, business cards of people I'd never contacted, bent paper clips and unclaimed student essays.

Five hundred more books on another wall awaited the boxes. The lower two-thirds of these shelves housed my large collection of biographies, many of them of doorstopper dimensions, and many of them unread, together with American literature texts and books about literary theory, and my library of Judaica, including hundreds of volumes of Australian Jewish autobiography, much of it Holocaust memoir, about which I had written a book.

As I packed I left a lot of unwanted books out on a laminex coffee table in the corridor, amazed each morning at how many had been scavenged the previous day by indigent and dedicated students, and by those who just scavenged for scavenging's sake. But many of the unread books were not exactly unwanted, despite the fact that when they arrived home to the new walls of shelving that were being installed as I packed, most of them would remain unread by this slow reader whose appetite for doorstoppers was waning by the day.

So what was *that* all about? A sort of comfort, I think: the feeling that this raw, dizzying thing called a life—Samuel Beckett calls it "the spray of phenomena"—could be lined by a vast but cozy conversation among inquiring people who wanted to know, maybe in some cases even *knew*, what it meant to live well, to flourish in a deeply human way. That's what I was after now; come to think of it, that's what I had always been after. The strange nuances of personal identity meant that I felt most myself in a room if it was lined with books because books and teaching had been identity-conferring, had been my trade.

Those on the brink of retirement often cling to work identity—however welcome release from workplace routines and politics might be—because that long-supported identity is under threat. And the clinging can continue well into the retired state. My fine workaholic father used early in retirement to put on suit and tie and drive into the city for appointments my mother knew did not exist.

I think there lurks also in the minds of many who arrive at this threshold the residue of a long-cherished hope: the hope of a belated but spectacular augmentation of personal capacity, a late and luxuriant blooming of one's potential. As Montaigne observes: "Our desires incessantly renew their youth." I hadn't quite given up on the dream of becoming a fast reader who might after all plough through a doorstopper in a day and write, not a Key to All Mythologies, but the Book that Shifted a Paradigm. I was shifting furniture out of an academic office.

The biographies were destined for new shelves in the rumpus room—the Man Cave, as we called it at home—in which Elliot held parties, played pool, and spread chaotic good cheer. There was no option: all the other wall space in the house that could reasonably be used for books was already occupied. I wondered how this arrangement would go and didn't entirely welcome the thought of my treasured volumes standing witness to teenage events.

And indeed in the mornings after Elliot's parties, there'd be beer bottles, liqueur bottles, stray iPhones, stubs of pool cue chalk, coins, and empty cigarette packets on the shelves beside my precious tomes. But the funny thing was—I didn't mind. I thought I would, but I didn't. I found it fun to wonder, for instance, why certain books had performed mysterious relocations during the inebriate night. Walt Whitman's collected poems once transited from the American literature wall, past the pool table, over a beanbag and came to rest on the opposite wall, among the literary theory books. I surmised it had something to do with the cover on that Whitman edition, featuring two naked men at a swimming hole, excerpted from Thomas Eakins' late-nineteenth-century painting "The Swimming Hole."

One afternoon, after Elliot and stragglers had made partial recoveries from the night before, I inquired of my bleary-eyed son what a particularly large doorstopper—Deidre Bair's biography of Samuel Beckett—was doing on the pool table. Had some of the kids studied *Waiting for Godot* at school, perhaps? No, he informed me, there was a less literary explanation: a girl had passed out on the pool table and they had propped her head on Bair's *Beckett* before conveying her to Madeleine's bed to sleep off her indisposition.

Some months later at Elliot's school graduation dinner, a tastefully attired young woman was making her way with her demure mother to a nearby table when, spotting us, she cupped her hands over a barely suppressed smile, and blushed.

"What's up with her?" I whispered to Elliot.

"Oh," he said, "that's the girl who passed out on the pool table."

And why not? In retirement I get a particular, if sometimes percussive kick, out of Joseph Heller's travesty of Shakespeare:

> Some men are born mediocre, some men achieve mediocrity, and some men have mediocrity thrust upon them.

Two

And what number do you wear, son?

It was mid-winter in Melbourne and yet again I was at home sick with my mother, Fleur. Bronchitis, sinusitis—the usual afflictions. I didn't greatly mind missing school—Fleur was fun company and endlessly attentive—but I did miss kicking the footy at recess and I found it humiliating not being able to join the pack of kids who played football in the park at the bottom of the street.

One wet late afternoon my father, Paul, strode with uncharacteristic jauntiness into the living room, sidled up to me and said with feigned offhandedness, "I don't suppose you'd like to meet Ron Barassi?"

He knew full well that no prospect could be closer to my six-year-old heart. I was a fanatical follower of the Melbourne Football Club, and Barassi, its vice-captain and star player, was more than an idol to me. He was a god. His famous number—31—was stitched in white plastic to the back of the Melbourne sweater I wore to the park, to matches, and even around the house. My other hero, Picasso, couldn't compare.

Barassi had an aura like few other athletes I've seen. Well

before other Australian footballers had begun scientifically sculpting their physiques in gyms, he had fashioned his hulking Italian-Australian physique into a thing of rippling explosive power. He had unusually long arms, a barrel-chest, massive thighs and a slightly ponderous gait that rocked from side to side as he walked or, rather, prowled the field like a great primate. But when he exploded into action he was all cohesive force and, though not particularly gifted at the game's more subtle arts, he had made himself into one of its highly skilled players by dint of extraordinary willpower. It was this—his phenomenal, all-consuming, unrelenting, almost demonic determination—which, more than anything, made his reputation and shaped his fabulously successful career as player, coach, and later commentator. A famous photo, his square Italian face, wavy hair and uncommonly wide mouth contorted with effort, shows him crashing through a tackle and launching a kick, arms flung akimbo, an opposition player trying desperately to pull him off his feet. Poet Tom Petsinis writes of him "grimacing revenge." Five decades on, I gaze up at a bronze statue fashioned from that photo—one of the "Legends" statues that ring the MCG—whenever I go to the football or cricket.

"*Huh*?!" I replied in disbelief. "Whaddya mean?"

"Well," my father continued, "I need new furniture in my office and, funnily enough, when I contacted a furniture company it turned out that its boss is Ron Barassi. So he's coming to do the job. Just thought I'd tell you as a matter of interest. No need to come and meet him if you don't feel like it."

"*Are you KIDDING?!*" I said, and it was arranged that my mother would drive me in to the office mid-morning the next day to meet the great man.

———

"Now, I think you might be the young man who's here to meet Barass." My father's chatty PA at the Gas and Fuel Corporation headquarters winked as we approached his office.

I don't think I said much because, having flown through breakfast in the most buoyant of spirits and insisting that we leave early to make sure I didn't miss my hero, I was now feeling oddly flat, more anxious than excited, even a touch queasy, as if my legs had become unsteady.

But "Barass"—the nickname had a reassuringly friendly ring to it, and it was used by friend and foe alike. A sporting hero of his stature had many friends, of course, but someone so ferociously competitive and success-obsessed was bound also to have enemies. And he did.

His father, Ron Snr, a fine Melbourne player, had been killed at Tobruk early in the war. This, it was said, had left a kind of emptiness in the son who bore his name, a sensation that he'd felt compelled to appease in everything he did, especially in his father's club colors.

My father, smartly attired in a dark suit and light tie, was deep in conversation on the phone when we came in, but I'd say he'd been waiting expectantly for Fleur and me in his distracted sort of way, because he wedged the receiver between chin and shoulder, pointed to his watch, held up five fingers and winked at me. Barass, Ron—or should it be

Mr. Barassi? I wondered—would be here in five minutes.

"It's not every day that the world's greatest footballer comes to kit out your office, is it?" said Paul, having put down the phone and emerged from behind his desk to give Fleur a peck on the cheek and me a gentle punch just below the right shoulder.

"Nope," I said, noting the surprisingly percussive bony impact of that affectionate gesture and feeling strangely defeated by what hadn't yet occurred.

Soon the PA knocked at the door, announced "Mr. Barassi is here to see you," and stepped away. There, filling almost the entire doorframe, was a huge leonine figure in a shiny silver suit, black shoes and smart thin tie. His dark wavy hair was brushed back, his blue eyes blazing with life, his mouth angled into a slightly lopsided business-like smile.

"Ron," said Paul, "I'd like you to meet a fan of yours and a great Melbourne follower—Richard Freadman."

The great man began to extend a hand but seeing no inclination in me to return his gesture he withdrew it and addressed me, now hovering half-hidden behind my mother: "G'day, Richard. And what number do you wear on your back, son?"

Since in those days it was customary for all men—or at least all who would qualify as a "man's man"—to address boys, even male adolescents, as "son," there was nothing particularly cordial in my hero's term of address. But this warm-hearted man, brimming with life and basking in the famous career he was carving out for himself, was doing his best, and he must have wondered why this "Richard" couldn't do better than reply, in a squeaky voice, peeking at him from behind his mother's waist: "Thirty-one."

I was so overcome that I don't recall what he said next. I think my father, perhaps a bit disappointed at my lack of manly confidence, covered for me, asking about the form of Melbourne's out-of-sorts centerman, Laurie Mithen.

And then it was down to business: Paul described to Ron what was wrong with the current configuration of the office and which items of furniture he'd like to dispense with; Ron paced and measured, then indicated where various new bits of furniture might stand, how much space they'd take, what manner of movement about the office they would allow if thus positioned, and what permutations would permit Paul a view out of the window into the busy street below. Since the occasion had switched so decisively from football to office furniture, and since I'd rendered myself all but invisible, I don't think my hero paid me much attention as he took his leave.

Trying in his kindly way to disguise his disappointment and to rekindle some of my excitement, my father said to me with feigned enthusiasm, "So how was *that*, young fella?!"

"Really good," I replied, seething at myself for my pathetic performance. I didn't want to be squeaking at "Barass" from behind my mother's skirt. I wanted to step forward, look him in his manly eyes, and shake his hand, hard. I wished I could re-run the tape. Next time I'd make an impression and give my father reason to be proud.

I wanted to go home now, put on my number 31 Melbourne sweater, burst through imaginary packs, and kick long goals in the park. Get the irky feelings out of my system and reclaim my fragile connection to manhood.

But this wasn't about to happen. Dr. John Coldbach, my pediatrician, cold by name and cold by nature, had been quite firm when passing a stethoscope over my lungs a couple of days before: "No outdoor exercise for a month."

Three

Cutting through

Something there is that doesn't love a wall

—Robert Frost, "Mending Wall"

That bloody fairway!

It was driving me nuts, this manicured nirvana just paces from our rear windows. We'd moved to reduce our mortgage and because we loved the view from the new kitchen, dining and living rooms, down the fourth fairway of the Eastern Golf Club, but for some odd reason I kept delaying my golfing debut.

There was nothing too exclusive about this establishment, its membership a cross-section of well-heeled multicultural Melbourne. A fifth-generation Australian-Anglo-Jew could waltz in—just find two nominators and write a $4000 check.

It seemed an odd thing to do when we'd just moved to cut our mortgage and drop to one income so that my wife, Diane, could help Madeleine through the final two years of high school—a tough time for any kid, let alone one suffering, as we were later to learn, from bipolar depression.

But at last I did it, and not without spousal encouragement. Golf, we thought, might moderate my addiction to work, might help me to relax. I was fifty-three and had been working like a dog for years. Yes, I needed to relax. In fact, I was absolutely determined to relax. I was going to bend my steely will in leisure's direction—right down that Edenic fairway.

I took a series of lessons with Mick, the Club pro, a laconic guide for the middle of the journey. The lessons were a birthday present from the family, who reasoned that if I knew how to play golf I'd find it more relaxing. Delighted with the gift, I was determined to make a real go of the game so that I could ease into middle age, amble carpeted fairways to the sweet calm of retirement.

Mick seemed just the man for me. He appeared to sense that I was the heady type—or was it the professorial title on the business card I gave him before the first lesson? There was a touch of Zen about Mick, whose First Rule of Golf was: "Don't watch the ball." A lifelong devotee of ball sports, I'd received plenty of advice in my time, but this was a first. "Don't watch the ball." Jesus! And a golf ball came second only to a squash ball as the smallest sporting object I'd ever tried to hit. A tennis ball looked like a pumpkin by comparison.

Mick added: "Golf's a very simple game." So sure was he about this that for one doubt-dispelling moment I believed him.

"All sorts of people will tell you all sorts of things but

99 percent of it is bullshit. There are a million ways to play good golf. It's just a matter of finding *your* way."

Well, fine, I thought. "But are you *sure* it would be counterproductive for me to watch the ball?"

Actually, his reasons for turning a blind eye to the ball were quite compelling. Golf, he explained, is about propelling something "out there" toward a target. People get so hung up on watching the ball they turn in on themselves. They get "too introspective." They get tense. They don't let the club head do the work. Being a compulsive self-scrutinizer, it occurred to me that this might not bode well.

He had the form to back these almost mystical understandings. "Watch this," he said, addressing the ball with bemusing ease. "Now I'll close my eyes."

Back and smoothly through came the club. A booming drive arced two hundred meters down the middle of the driving range fairway. A shot played as if by a god—by a man with his eyes closed!

Fair enough, I thought. I'm too tense anyway. This will force me to relax. So I took that bit of advice together with another of his tips: "Swing the club all the way back until it's brushing your left shoulder blade, and then all the way through until it's brushing your right one." A full, fluid swing. That was the thing.

I'm a very determined person. I need to do things well. Even when I'm doing them in order to relax. The scent of success mollifies my twitchy Jewish nostrils, and many years ago I had been deeply impressed by legendary football coach Ron Barassi, when he proclaimed with Delphic circularity that "Practice doesn't make perfect. *Perfect practice* makes perfect!" So armed with this and Mick's injunctions, I set about executing perfect practice in pursuit of perfection, chipping plastic balls in the family courtyard, hitting buckets of yellow balls at the driving range. It was relaxing, getting the feel of the club, anticipating the sweet kiss of blade on glistening puckered white orb, the ethereal arc after effortless mellifluous motion.

Actually, over the years, playing the occasional social game I hadn't been too bad. But now, despite Mick's laconic desiderata, I was plunged into the torments of sporting preposterousness. Huge drives, aimed at distant targets, the ball, quite incidental to the club's magnificent pendular *whoosh*, would trickle off at absurd angles, coming to rest fifteen meters away, at fifty, sixty, even eighty-five degrees to its intended line of flight. Blessed with better than average hand-eye coordination, I was now playing like a man with motor neuron disease. I was stunned. Infuriated. Humiliated. My back hurt. I was not relaxed.

Witnessing my misery from a neighboring tee, a kindly man of my age said: "Like a couple of hints?"

I did not demur.

"Where did you get that swing?" he asked.

"I've been having some lessons from the Club pro."

"Oh, you mean Mick?"

"That's right."

"Yeah. I had some lessons from Mick once. He gave me a lovely smooth swing. It felt great. Balance. Rhythm. Let the club do the work. Don't worry about the ball.

Just think about where it's going. Problem was, it hardly went anywhere. It took me six months to get the club face reacquainted with the ball."

He gave me a few pointedly un-Mick-like tips. "The pros don't take the club head all the way back, so why should you? He's got you collapsing your left knee. You should be able to swing with a basketball between your knees. Keep your head over the ball."

My improvement was marked and immediate. I was on my way, "my nerves were brass or hammer'd steel"—and to hell with Mick!

Funnily enough, in the last of my lessons with Mick – this time playing a few holes on the main course—I felt I should comply with his earlier teachings. Again I played like a dog. Now, apparently convinced that I was beyond help, Mick changed tack. Encouragement modulated into consolation: "You know, you don't have to be hitting great shots all the time to enjoy golf. You've got beautiful scenery, you can chat with friends, and the medicos reckon a good walk beats the hell out of jogging."

Get stuffed, Mick! I muttered inwardly.

That was it for golf. Bugger it! And as for the $4000 joining fee—too bloody bad! We still had that divine view down the fourth fairway.

But that *bloody* fairway! No sooner would my gaze repose there than I'd think of the fee—money down the goddamned drain!—and Mick, with his decisive, priestly, disastrous intervention in my life, extolling the cardiovascular and interpersonal dividends of walking.

And now something entirely unexpected happened. Diane offered to play a few holes with me. We just did it. No score cards, no worries. Just enjoy the scenery and swing. She surprised herself by hitting the ball with some regularity. Studiously ignoring Mick's tuition, I started to play the occasional good shot. And occasional is all you need; any weekend hack will tell you that. So sweet is that occasionally crisp kiss of club face on ball, the sight of it sailing into the green yonder farther than you thought you could ever hit it, that you keep coming back for more. Golf's addictive rhythms.

Soon I was playing a few holes after work. Alone, with no card, no score, no intention of finishing the course, I started to enjoy myself. To relax. On a gentle incline beside the second fairway, where my ball had come to rest in stubbly native grass, I saw the error of my ways: I'd been making golf another project in a life already burdened with projects, objectives, benchmarks, commitments, inauthentic criteria of worthiness and distinction. I needed not to give a shit about being really good at golf: just to stroll those lovely tree-lined fairways and pristine greens, fiddling with my swing at leisure, enjoying the occasional good shot and not worrying about the others. Though still cranky with Mick, I was surprised to find myself deferring to some of his folksy insights: "There are a million ways to play good golf. It's just a matter of finding *your* way."

I tried a few things: shortish backswing; keeping both feet planted; not too much give in the left knee; simplifying everything; orienting myself toward and picturing the

41

target—yes—but allowing myself to watch the ball if I felt the need; letting the club flow through the ball.

Things started to improve. I was having fun. I'd got the bug. Diane, who sometimes joined me, was enjoying it too.

———

The back fence, which gleamed new and formidable, was too high for a man of my age and limited dexterity to scale. But it seemed absurd that in order to play we had to drive half a kilometer around the perimeter of the course, cross a major arterial road, and leave the car in the Club car park. The more so because immediately to the right of our house there was an easeway onto the course with two padlocked gates for maintenance vehicles. If only I could get a key to those gates! But it was against Club regulations.

My one "in" at the Club, Phil Wong, an irreverent knockabout Chinese-Australian who'd nominated me, reckoned he could talk the greenkeeper into cutting me a copy of the key. At a barbecue a claret-emboldened Phil outlined his mode of approach to this holder of high horticultural office. He'd take him aside, explain my pained and worthy situation, and appeal to their long history of larrikin solidarity at the Club.

But it didn't work. An uncharacteristically subdued Phil had later to explain that the greenkeeper was "crook" on him about something, and it was a no go. Why not just have a gate installed? I reminded him of the emails from the Club containing stern injunctions against using gates onto the course—even by members. I checked the legalities with the local council: gates onto golf courses, like gates between neighbors' fences, are a civil matter, to be negotiated by the two parties. But I knew the Club wouldn't come to the table. Its *Club Syllabus* was a dead ringer for that of St Andrews, Scotland, home of golf: pages and pages of arcane regulations. Another document, bearing the deceivingly convivial title "Welcome to New Members" lists among its many prohibitions: "Ladies shorts not extending to within 100 mm of the knee." T-shirts must have collars; no logos other than the Club's on any apparel. And so on. Anyway, a gate was going to cost another $500.

Then it occurred to me that a gate wasn't necessary. All I needed was a secret trapdoor-like entry in the fence though which I could walk straight onto the course with a few clubs and balls, and practice on the fourth fairway and green. I'm no handyman but I reckoned I could do it, and cheaply too—under $10 instead of $500. So I purchased two long bolts and butterfly nuts. I had an assortment of cheap tools, screws, nails, and a ladder under the house. I borrowed a cordless drill from a neighbor, and waited for the cover of darkness.

———

It had been a beautiful autumnal Melbourne day: crisp, calm, balmy.

At seven-thirty, nicely primed by dinner, I carried the standard lamp from the dining room down the garden path beside the house and positioned it by the fence, assembled my collection of tools, and set about executing my plan—a plan so elegant, simple, and meticulously thought through that I reckoned on being back inside to watch *On the Couch*, a weekly football post-mortem, by nine.

—∽∞∽—

With Peanut the cat in attendance things started well. I began working on a small, three-slatted section right at the end of the fence, where the crossbeams jutted for twenty-five centimeters from the last post, resting on air. The plan was to remove the slats, nail them together with connecting horizontal timber, cut them in half, nailing the top half back to the fence. The bottom half would be a lift-outable trapdoor that fastened and unfastened to the crossbeams by the bolts I'd bought. It would just be a matter of screwing and unscrewing the butterfly nuts, lifting the panel in and out, and perhaps securing it at the bottom with a padlock when not in use.

The twenty-five-centimeter section of pelmet atop the fence lifted off easily enough. Various wrenchings and hammer clunks freed the palings from their beams. I was so focused on the task I only half-noticed the occasional drops of rain. But it didn't matter: at that rate I'd easily make *On the Couch*. Might even have time for a shower beforehand.

Fiddly tasks like this are all about foresight. Check everything at each stage before moving on to the next. In the planning stage I'd leant against the appointed section of the fence to check that I'd be able to fit through the gap I was going to create. It looked tight but about right. Side-on, I'd be able to glide on and off the course in seconds.

Savoring the vindication that would come with my

first slither onto that neighboring wonderland, I turned sideways, lifted my left leg through, bent down to enable my torso to fit between the middle and lower crossbeams, and pushed. About mid-way, my potbelly and barrel-chest wedged rib-crackingly against either side of the aperture, the lower crossbeam setting crippling limits to my intended stoop.

And then it started to rain. Hard. It was bucketing down. My top was immediately drenched. My old track shoes, likewise soaked, started to churn mud in that southeast corner. The mud didn't smell all that good. It must have been a bit like this as Virgil and Dante passed out of Hell via Satan's rectum. But that was the least of my problems.

I squeezed out and stood there in the driving rain, pondering my next move.

One thing was clear. I couldn't leave the job half-done, because vigilant players and groundsmen would be on the course at first light. If they saw a gap in the fence they'd report it immediately to the Club. I couldn't sleep on that prospect. I'd have nightmares about appearing before the Eastern Golf Club Disciplinary Sub-Committee, standing guiltily before them in ladies shorts not extending to within a hundred millimeters of the knee. And I had hairy legs!

Diane had witnessed enough of my handyman endeavors over the years to give this covert operation a wide berth, but as I stood there in the rain, contemplating the misfit between me and the gap I'd created, a kitchen window slid open and with nicely feigned good cheer she inquired: "How's it going?"

"Good," I said. "I've got the pelmet up and the palings off. But there is a bit of a problem."

"What's that?"

"I can't quite fit though the gap."

"*Right.*"

"Wanna come and give an opinion?"

"Not really."

"Wanna come anyway?"

Eventually she made her way down the garden path and after dismayed assessment suggested that I re-attach the section I'd removed and create a bigger one to the right of the last post. Elliot, age nine, had come with her and wandered into the fray with all the acuity of Tolstoy's Pierre Bezukhov in *War and Peace* who, seeking the battlefield, is quite unaware that he has stumbled into it. Elliot launched an attack on the fence with a variety of tools in what seemed to be an entirely random manner. He is one of life's great enthusiasts, but I was in no mood for engagements with the fence that were even more grossly amateur than my own. Wisely, Diane returned to the house, taking him with her.

Without restoring the original palings, I tried to loosen the next lot along to make more room, but they didn't want to budge, and I'd make a real mess of the fence if I kept widening the gap. The alternative was to cut the lower crossbeam that traversed the gap so that I could stoop low enough to ram my torso through the hole.

The rain continued to bucket down. Peanut had re-treated to a dry spot under the eaves, emitting mews of I'm not sure what. Concern? Disbelief? Hilarity? With cats it's hard to know. The dogs, on the other hand, were clearly delighted to have me out there in their whiffy, turdy, bone-strewn domain. The elderly black bitzer, Leo, wagged be-nignly up at me. Haggis, the exuberant schnoodle puppy, hurtled about, periodically hanging off my dripping sleeves.

As we know, major initiatives have defining moments. Having severed the lower crossbeam, I had arrived at one such moment: if I could not get though the gap now my entire scheme was in ruins, and I'd mutilated our fine new fence for naught.

Gingerly, I started to lower myself again, my right shoe twisting in the now conspicuously stinky mud. What *is* that stench? I wondered. And then I remembered … Shortly af-ter we moved in, the toilets started to misbehave. Walking the perimeter of the house, torch in hand, I found sewage oozing from an overflow pipe, running down the concrete path beside the house, and settling in the southeast corner of the yard.

I now knew myself to be under multiple threats: from the Club, the rain, raw sewage, and perhaps even the constabulary, who might at any moment be summoned by concerned neighbors.

No point in getting any more drenched, I thought. So I trudged inside to put on a dry t-shirt and a waterproof anorak. As I passed the bedroom, the family, reclining on our bed, watching the Eurovision Song Competition, asked how it was going.

"Slowly," I replied.

— ∞ —

There were other impediments. Between the southeast corner of the yard and the underneath area of the house, where my tools were kept, sat Madeleine's trampoline. Since it was Olympic-sized, if I needed anything from under the house I had to edge along the fence's middle crossbeam, or scramble like an arthritic sea lion over the trampoline's wet plunging surface, or crawl under it—a maneuver that Haggis immediately construed as an invitation to play.

But obstacles had to be overcome. It was now 11 p.m. The job had to be done.

Kneeling sideways and expelling air to render myself as svelte as possible, I again addressed the gap. Right shoe twisting, I levered myself in and pushed ... and pushed, and pushed. About halfway I began to fear for my rib cage and to envision morning headlines:

**DONCASTER FATHER OF THREE SURVIVES
STORMY NIGHT WEDGED IN FENCE**

My anorak's slitheriness was in my favor and finally, after expelling still more air, I pushed again and was rebirthed onto the Eastern Golf Course, drenched, disoriented but vindicated. I was now in quite good spirits.

I'd gotten used to the rain and was quite pleased at the harm it seemed unable to do me. *On the Couch* was now well and truly over, Diane certainly wasn't going to come near me, and the dawn I so feared was still many hours off.

I was free to hack and tinker away with my dripping tools, supermarket torch in hand, until I'd achieved my goal. Later, in consultation with my neighbor, I could slightly widen the aperture by relocating one of the palings on our dividing fence.

The dogs were in good spirits too, availing themselves of the wonderland beyond the fence, hitherto merely sniffed from the yard. The most ardent golfer could not be more enamored of that fourth fairway than Leo and Haggis. Soon Peanut joined them. So there we all were, oblivious to the rain, sloshing about in our benighted suburban oasis. An observer might have reckoned our collective IQ at about ninety-five.

There was still work to be done—plenty of it, given that it takes me three tries to do anything with my hands. Nailing the upper section back in place seemed easy enough—until I found that it didn't leave room for the lower section to edge in beneath it and rest on the pelmet at the foot of the fence. So off again it had to come for further modifications.

It was odd out there, ten meters from the family home's secure glow, but with one's back to this vastness, ringed though it was by lights from neighboring houses. What manner of man or beast might prowl these immaculate acres at night? Foxes, feral cats (the lynx of the links?), dingoes, ravenous refugees from the fossil records, spotted leopards, Woody Allen's "wheat-germ killers"? Same-sex psychopaths who roam the darkened greens and fairways, preying upon unsuspecting middle-aged academics hacking away by torchlight in the rain at suburban fences?

A rustle in the long grass between fairway and fence spun me about, my torch beam scanning the undergrowth for skulking monstrosities, but finding only Leo's cataract-clouded eyes glowing milkily in the glare. Haggis flew at my sleeve. Reassured, I continued.

But really, what was this all about? Wasn't there something a touch desperate about this hacking at a barrier between desire and pleasure? *How very me!* How very male. Having begun, I had to finish; but not just on account of the Club autocrats—as I well knew, there were lots of nice and forgiving folk in the Club and, indeed, on the committees. No, once I begin something I *always* have to finish it. It's as if I've put down a deposit on a satisfaction that I think will at last appease my gnawing inner disquiet.

I'd left a container of nails on the central heating unit beside the trampoline. I was reluctant to barge my way back into the yard, but I did need more nails in order to finish, that is to say *really finish*, the job in every imagined detail. So back I rib-crackingly went, squelching in the murk like a suburban Ciacco.

The kitchen window slid open again. This time it was Madeleine, an inveterate bouncer at sixteen years of age, who will only use her trampoline at night when there's nobody on the fairway or green to see her mop of lustrous curly black hair rising and dipping above the fence line. At such times we have to vacate the back of the house because she doesn't like being watched by us either.

"How's it going?"

"Slowly, but I'm getting there."

"How long do you think it will take now?"

"Not sure. Why?"

"Well, I'd like to bounce, but not with you there."

"Darlin', you've just been in bed for two days with a cold and it's pissing down with rain. No bouncing tonight."

"But I'll wear a thick waterproof coat—the one you got in New York when you were a student."

"Maddie, no nagging, *please!* This is taking much longer than I expected and I'm drenched."

"Why not finish it tomorrow?"

"Because the t-shirt police will chuck me in the cooler."

"Whaddya mean?"

"I'll tell you later."

"So how much longer, Dad?"

"Jeez, I don't know. Maybe forty minutes. I'll tell you when I'm done, and actually it won't be hard to tell because I'll come in the minute I'm finished. I'm not planning to sleep in the rain."

The window slid closed.

I put the nails in a pocket and took the neighbor's drill this time, re-birthing myself again onto the links. I now had to drill two holes in the trapdoor and through the crossbeam. Through these holes I'd thread the bolts that would fasten the hatch to the fence, secured by the butterfly bolts from the inside. All I'd have to do is unscrew the bolts, push the hatch outwards, slip through, replace the hatch, and stroll onto the fairway.

After the usual mistakes and re-tries the job was done. The bolts slipped into place; I knocked the hatch into position, lifted it out again, and whistled for the dogs. Haggis flew through the gap; the rotund, arthritic Leo wriggled his way through.

I maneuvred the hatch into position. But how would I thread the bolts through their holes from the inside? *Jesus!* Eventually I found that I could coax them through from under the crossbeam, but with enormous difficulty. And it took ten minutes. In order to get the hatch snugly into place I had to scale the fence and tap it firmly with a hammer from the other side. So there would have to be some fine-tuning the next day after all.

Still, the thing was basically done! It had taken over four and half hours, but it had sort of worked. The pets were back in the yard and I wasn't *all that* cold. I felt a faint glimmer of satisfaction and made my way up the garden path, back into the light. The rain ha ceased. Stars twinkled high above the fairway trees. Thence to the shower where I vigorously disinfected my hands with Dettol.

"Are you done yet?" Madeleine called from outside the door.

"Yes, dear."

"*Yay!*"

Postscript

Some years later, after the trapdoor had given excellent but increasingly uncomfortable service, I did indeed install a hinged gate, hidden by a tree that had shot up near our fence. In June 2015 the Eastern Golf Club relocated to a new course thirty minutes away, and an international construction company commenced work on a vast residential development that would eventually plonk a two-story house where our fairway view had been.

Four

The bigger you are, the harder they fall

When I was a child, I spake as a child, I understood as a child; but when I became a man, I put away childish things.

—1 Corinthians 13:11 (KJV)

———

At six foot four and 220 pounds he could seem a scary guy. But Elliot is more basking shark than white pointer. McDuff the terrier's tail thrashes wildly when he hears Elliot's leisurely, benign footfall in the gray slate hallway. Elli is benign. His gray-blue eyes are sleepy but astute, his round face well contoured for a smile. People are pleased to hear him coming too.

Elliot was my fourteen-year-old sports-loving son. He'd play and watch pretty much anything, but his introduction to Aussie Rules football was a disappointment. Soon after he started playing he joined a very good team and found himself on the reserve bench in a grand final. His coach, a red, gnome-faced bundle of muscle with a patchy short beard that lapped at his cheekbones, was familiar with the principle of giving all the kids plenty of game time. But he wasn't about to sacrifice success to that principle—certainly not in a grand final—and so he would beckon Elliot from the bench, sending him into gratifyingly important positions from which a boy might shape the destiny of the game, only to haul him back off immediately on the pretext of some sudden strategic exigency. The bewildered and betrayed look on Elli's face as the runner escorted him from the field was painful to behold, and as he jogged the victory lap with the team, club banner and trophy aloft, I could see that he was feigning elation.

It must be admitted that Elli lacked mobility on the Aussie Rules football field, a fact not unrelated to his love of fun and food (and, no doubt, his genetic makeup). When I raised the fitness issue—with all the tact and indirection I could muster—he took it in his easygoing stride and said he'd work on it. Somehow he never quite got round to it, but luckily his Aussie Rules career did not suffer—that was the last game he ever played.

He decided to concentrate on his other sporting love, basketball. Here his formidable physique worked for him, as he rebounded from defense, grabbing the ball and spearing passes to teammates, or loitering near the key, and potting lay-ups with a regularity that often ensured victory. Even here, though, his fitness was tested as he trundled from one end of the court to the other. Late in a game he'd be laboring. He needed to be fitter and more combative to move up a grade next season. But did he want to make the effort?

He started jogging at night and lifting weights at school. When Diane heard about a former US and Australian basketballer, Phil Smart, who did one-on-one coaching nearby, we asked Elli if he was interested. "*Sweet!*" he said. "When can I start?" I rang Phil who suggested that we meet in the Doncaster McDonald's the following Sunday at 6 p.m.

⸻

As you approach that McDonald's you pass Elliot's Chinese restaurant of choice, the Golden Dragon Palace, followed by the inevitable Kentucky Fried Chicken then, rounding out Doncaster's multicultural ambience, Macedon Square, with its Greek and Italian cafes. We arrived at McDonald's a few minutes early and chose a table.

"I'm starving," said Elli, fresh from a long afternoon on the sofa.

"Bud," I said, "I guess it wouldn't be a great look to be tucking into a Big Mac when Phil turns up."

"Yeah, I guess not."

A few minutes later Phil rang to say that he was just around the corner. He'd been at a seminar that had finished late. I could see that Elli was on edge, his eyes flitting between the food queue and the main door. I felt strangely apprehensive too, hoping that Phil would be kindly with Elli and that the meeting would go well. Elli was a big boy, but he was only fourteen, after all.

Eventually a tall, upright, shimmering figure appeared in the foyer. The fluorescent lights glinted off his shaved black head and tinted steel-rimmed glasses; his lean frame was wrapped in a double-breasted silver suit, a metallic silver tie set immaculately against a black shirt. He had huge hands and feet.

I felt oddly unmanly when he shook my hand hard and looked me straight in the eye. "You must be Dick," he said in a deep unwavering voice and then, shifting his attention, "And you must be Elliot, right?"

"Right," said the awestruck Elli.

As we were sitting down I asked whether Phil would like anything to eat or drink. "Not for me," he said, "I'm in trainin'." He explained that he was preparing for the Veterans' World Basketball Championships. He'd played in the national league in Australia, but not in the NBA in the US. This was his chance to test himself against the best, albeit the best past their prime. "I don't wanna die wondering," he said. "This is my last chance."

Behind his back the food queue had grown longer.

"Yeah, this is the fittest I've ever bin. I'm trainin' with the former Miss World. She's got me working out five hours a day and watching every calorie that passes my lips. This is serious, man. No second chance."

I was wondering what Elliot was making of the Miss World reference when Phil fixed him with one of his man-to-man stares.

"So, Elliot, what's your basketball dream?"

Elli paused, perhaps checking to see if in fact he had such a dream. "Well, I'd like to improve enough to move up to A-Grade."

"And then what?" Phil shot back.

"I dunno really. Maybe play in a higher league."

"And *then* what?"

Elli wasn't often stuck for words but just now they weren't coming very readily.

"You're a big guy," said Phil, "almost as tall as me. How old are you?"

"Fourteen."

"Man, you're fourteen and six foot four! You might hit six eight, or even seven feet. Then we're talking American college ball—maybe more!"

Of course Elli, like any kid, had talked idly about being the next Michael Jordon, though without any great conviction. But here was a shining silver emissary from Basketball Heaven lighting a path to sporting stardom!

"So, man, you gotta have a dream. And then you gotta work, work, work for it! Man, I live for basketball. I got a job in the car industry but that's just to pay the bills. I eat 'n' drink basketball and if you wanna come with me you gotta want it as bad as me. You gotta nail those skills and get really fit, not an ounce of fat on your body, just like Miss World is making me."

He paused and looked straight at Elli. "So how bad do you want it, Elliot?"

Pause. "Very bad," mumbled the boy. And then, "I *really* want it!"

"Alright, *deal!*" said Phil reaching across the table and shaking Elli's hand.

I was nearing sixty and feeling my years. I'd been fiercely competitive at sport as a boy, but nowadays a few holes of golf and a stroll in the park with the dogs were about my limit. But even I felt roused by the challenge this stranger had put to my son—bidding him to dream, strive and fulfill every ounce of his potential. I felt that even *I* might run through a brick wall for Phil, albeit a papier-mâché one.

Elli drew himself up straight and laid clenched fists on the table. He was seriously stirred. We talked arrangements. Phil said that practice courts were hard to find but he'd speak to a few people he knew. I said I'd check the availability of the courts at my university and at a local school. We'd tee something up and get everything underway in the next couple of weeks.

"So, matey boy," I said when Phil had gone, "what did you think of *that!?*"

"*Awesome!*"

"Still want Maccas for dinner?" I winked and nudged him in the ribs.

"*No way!* Let's go home and I'll ask Mum to cook me a steak."

Weeks passed. I couldn't find a court and Phil was always "caught up" and would get back to me. I wondered how Miss World felt about all those meetings and seminars.

Elli had changed his diet and started regular exercise, but the delay took the gloss off his determination. When I suggested that Miss World probably wasn't a pizza fan, he wearily replied, "When Phil finds a court, I'll start getting fit, Dad."

Eventually a text message arrived: "Hey Dick. If Elliot

still wants coaching a friend of mine called Jay Timbone is available. He's excellent. Played NBA. Call him on his cell phone. Phil."

"Sweet," said Elli when I told him. But by now another sporting dream had taken root where basketball had begun to flower.

He'd been tossing an American football about with friends at school for a while and we'd bought him a cheap Chinese-made imitation for Christmas. Watching the American game on cable TV, he'd decided that he wanted to try it.

He'd even done a sort of dream-calculation, an assessment of his chances of making it into the Australian gridiron team. The calculation went like this:

By the time I'm old enough to play seniors there will be eight sides in the Victorian League.

That = eight starting Centers in the Victorian League.

Two Centers will make the Victorian team = 25 percent chance of playing for Victoria for me.

Five Australian states have league standard gridiron teams = a total of ten Centers which can make the Australian team.

So if I make the Victorian team (25 percent chance), then I've got a 20 percent chance of making the Australian team after that.

These were far better odds than he could expect in Aussie Rules. In fact, aside from a group of players handpicked to play a hybrid Australian-Gallic code against Ireland, Australian football doesn't have a national team. Elliot had also concluded that hyper-strategic gridiron is "more intellectual" than our indigenous game.

Despite these undeniably compelling statistics I was unenthused—brutal game, another weekend commitment for Diane who was already exhausted by the end of her corporate working week—and I guessed that nothing would come of it. But Diane reckoned that if he'd play his part in organizing it we should support him.

Organize it he did: on the internet he found the home base and training times for the Croydon Rangers and bus times to the ground, and presented himself, *sans* parents, in his school uniform, at training that week. After a brief try-out the coach asked: "How old are you?"

"Fourteen," said Elliot.

"*You beauty!*" cried the coach, clearly short of boys in this age group.

Next I knew I was writing a registration check and handing him my credit card so that he could order gloves and a proper ball from America via the internet.

A few days later, sitting at the kitchen table, I heard clattering footsteps in the hallway. I looked up to see a colossus in silver-gray leggings, killer-robot fanned shoulder pads, black boots, and with curly light-brown hair jutting from beneath a silver helmet, eyes peering through the steel mesh of the visor with feigned ferocity. Haggis, our medium-sized schnoodle who was on hind legs, supplicating for attention from the behemoth, could only paw at its thigh pads.

"*Holy shit!*" I exclaimed. "*My God!*"

"Check the helmet, Dad," he said, taking it off and handing me an accessory that seemed to weigh more than my car.

"Jeez, El, how can you play in a thing like that?"

"Easy, Dad, you hardly know it's there once it's on."

———

That evening I was out in the courtyard, my battered paperback copy of Jack Nicklaus' *The Best Way To Better Golf* on the teak table beside me. Analyzing my swing's reflection in the courtyard's ten-foot windows, I was paying particular attention to my left elbow, which tended to "fold" before impact with the ball, causing loss of distance and other sources of golfing heartache.

Elliot appeared with a sheet of A4 paper, a carpenter's steel measuring tape, and a spool of silver duct tape. His American football was tucked under one arm. He proceeded to tape the paper to the brick wall about five or six feet up.

"Did you take a few blows to the head before they gave you the helmet?" I asked.

"No, I'm practicing my snaps."

"Your what?"

"Snaps, Dad. I'm playing Center. That's the guy that crouches down and then flicks the ball up to the Quarterback. I'm practicing getting the right spin and the right height for our Quarterback who's five two."

So there we were, father and son, honing our sporting skills in the courtyard, the dogs tranquilly savaging their marrowbones under the magnolia trees.

The drive to Rangers headquarters is quintessential outer-suburban Melbourne. A freeway takes you through a tunnel named Mullum Mullum, its entrance adorned with Aboriginal motifs, its inbound lane named for Dame Nelly Melba, the famous soprano. You veer off the freeway onto a bypass that conducts you through an increasingly green and open landscape to a more countrified road. You pass a vast American-style mall, the occasional petrol station, a big public hospital, the odd set of shops and then, on your right, nestling in rustic seclusion, the Le Pine Funeral Parlour.

"You reckon we should make a booking for you there, El?" I said as this last landmark came into view. "Gridiron's an incredibly rough game, isn't it? And you're playing in a fourteen-to-eighteen age group."

"I'm sure we won't be needing Le Pine," laughed Diane, though she too was wondering how Elli would fare against eighteen-year-olds.

"Very funny, Dad," said Elli. "So who's got the gray hair in this car? And anyway, gridiron's no rougher than Aussie Rules and in Aussie Rules you don't have protection. Also, I'm in the safest position on the field: the Center just has to block. He doesn't tackle. He just protects the Quarterback. Plus I'm as big as most of the older guys."

Soon, the ground appeared. Lined with pine trees and featuring a dilapidated brick clubhouse, it was scruffy but still not a bad vista for the houses and apartments across the road. In other directions the eye could travel long through parks and neighboring playing fields, and off to the Dandenong Ranges an hour away.

We met the head coach, Ricky, a laid-back comfortable man in his early thirties—the sort of coach whose confidence and good humor calms and emboldens his charges. Tommy, the defense coach, was a more angular, driven presence, hunched and tense in his movements, but good-humored all the same. Both were apparently seasoned senior players. I liked the tone they set—rigorous, businesslike, supportive, earthy, funny. Just right for a keen new arrival like Elli.

Diane and I stood on the sideline and watched practice. At one point the Quarterback threw a long pass to a Wide Receiver. The kid caught it and dashed, high stepping wide toward the boundary to avoid oncoming traffic. He was hurtling a few yards away from us when four bodies came down on him, smashing—and I mean *smashing*—him into the turf. The clash of helmets and the thud of bodies made me wince. Diane and I exchanged an anxious glance.

My mind circled back to the many years when I played a brutal contact sport, and without the protection that saw these Croydon kids jump briskly to their feet after a clash. It was hard to believe now. The last sporting risk I'd taken was on a tennis court a few years earlier, when I threw myself at a low forehand volley. I could feel my rigid aging torso tumbling, as if in slow motion, toward the red clay. I was powerless to break my fall and lay there stunned, not so much by the impact as by my walrus-like immobility.

But Elli was loving every minute of it. Part of his job

was to call the offence together after each play. Up would shoot his arm and this new kid would roar "*Huddle!*" They'd cluster around him, then take up positions, Elliot squatting with apparent confidence before snapping to the Quarterback. The snaps seemed to be going OK, so far as I could tell, but I was less confident about his blocks. Sometimes he seemed to paw at oncoming players the way drinkers shadow-box with tame kangaroos outside country pubs. Did he have the aggression necessary for this brutal game?

Even he was wondering about this. On the way home he told us that the next game would be against the Monash Warriors and that he'd be up against Mitch Ladden, the best player of any age in the country. Apparently Ladden played both seniors and juniors and was off to play college football for the University of Hawaii as soon as the Australian season was over.

"Well," said Diane, "it wouldn't hurt to work on your fitness for guys like that, would it?"

"Maybe," he said, "but the game's next week and, anyway, it's mainly about size. The Center doesn't have to run much. The main thing I've got to do is push hard and high near the guy's shoulder pads when he runs at me. I've got to shove him off balance so that he can't get at the Quarterback."

Ladden was indeed a colossus. He was six foot eight and had frightening explosive power in his enormous legs. As he eyeballed Elli, Le Pine flashed into my mind, but the snap found its mark. In the ensuing maelstrom, Ladden, playing both offence and defense, was wandering about as if supervising a training drill. As Ricky said later, "He wasn't even trying." Occasionally, though, he'd do something that made a mockery of the proceedings. He'd push Elli aside as if shifting a dining room chair. He'd shove a Rangers player so hard that he'd cannon into other players, sending them flying like skittles. Presumably because Ladden wasn't really trying, Croydon held a comfortable lead at halftime.

In the second half, the great man seemed to have decided that enough was enough. He bulldozed through a pack a few yards out for a touchdown. And then, in the next offensive play, he collected the ball on the twenty-yard line, put his head down and simply surged forward, opposition players hanging off him like men scrabbling for the doors of a moving minibus. The game was all but gone … and then … Ladden was helped off with a broken collarbone. Croyden regrouped and the game was theirs.

— ❦ —

Things were proceeding in the Freadman sporting household. My golf swing had improved a little but I'd aggravated an old hip injury by trying for too much rotation, and would need a layoff. Elliot had joined a basketball team at school with which he played a weekly game. ("How'd ya go, Bud?" I asked him when he came home after one game. "We won, but only because the other team didn't turn up," he said with no sign of vexation.) His gridiron gloves, which were too small, had popped and popped again even after the ministrations of a local Chinese seamstress. He ordered another pair from the US, only to later announce that they'd been chewed by the lawn mower on the ground in Croydon.

"You don't say," I remarked. "I wonder how that could have happened?"

"Don't worry, Dad," he said. "The Center in the Seniors says that you get a better grip without gloves anyway."

At his age I'd have been spitting chips about the gloves. But he wasn't like me, and he was still back there, in that balmy place where just about everything is fresh, fascinating and fun.

Refracted through my more turbulent soul, I can remember snatches of that place—the smell of linseed oil on my cricket bat, hours at an easel trying to paint like Picasso, the rustle of early erotic attraction. But somewhere along the way, a long way back, I started passing on fun in pursuit of some nameless, deeper, or more profound satisfaction, "that imagined 'otherwise' which is our practical heaven," as George Eliot puts it.

Elli wasn't always a model kid. He could nag like the best of them for whatever might be the next fun thing to do. I knew I yielded too readily to his demands, but better to nurture his gift for pleasure than set limits that might mirror the depths of my own emotional sobriety. Of course, he himself was a great source of fun for his sober old Dad.

⸺≈≈⸺

The Rangers had lost only one game and were destined for the Vic Bowl—the competition grand final. They were certain to meet the Warriors and—best news of the lot—Ladden would not be fit to play. Their biggest enemy now was complacency, but the team was confident that it would not set in. "*No way!*" Elli assured me.

And so the big day arrived. The gray skies and intermittent rain did little to dampen the country-fair atmosphere on the sidelines. As usual there was a sausage sizzle beside the canteen. We chatted with a Samoan dad whose son played linebacker in the team, and with local parents who were as surprised as us to have sons playing this foreign code. Teenage girls hung about smoking, chattering, and checking their mobiles. Dogs on leads inclined their moist twitching snouts toward the barbeque. Neighbors watched from their verandahs. The field was ringed by cars. Up on the terraced roofless stand, a surprisingly deep and professional Yankee voice was booming from a loudspeaker tethered to the railings and wrapped in a bin liner against the rain—a commentator, setting the scene. When he took a break, rock music shook the bin liner and the girls bopped in the breeze. We had Elli to thank for this new vista in our middle-aged lives.

When at last the game got underway, Croydon came with a rush. At halftime, with a score line of 26–0, our chicken rolls, Coke Zero and Christmas mince pies were tasting just fine, but in the second half the Warriors hit back hard. Two touchdowns and a conversion: 26–14. Then another touchdown, but it was disallowed on a technicality. Croydon looked flat. They'd relaxed—complacency?—and seemed unable to find the fire again. Another Warrior surge. But then, on the next offensive play, Elliot snapped true to the Quarterback whose long spiraling pass pierced the late-afternoon mist. The Wide Receiver gathered, skipped sideways to avoid lunging defenders, darted wide and—"*touchdown!*" 32–14. Diane and I didn't know how much time was left, but when Rangers' players tipped a keg of ice water over Ricky's head, we figured we were home.

When the siren sounded the team ran toward the Quarterback. I saw Elli running flat out toward the pack. He launched and crashed in, as did teammates from other angles. Then the group reached skywards, a tepee of arms, Elli on tiptoe, straining to get his hand as high as it could go.

As the players received their Vic Bowl medallions and then gathered under the Rangers flag for photos, I felt a lump rise in my throat. I smudged away tears with the back of my hand. Elli had made all this happen in three short months. What a sunny kid he was and how he deserved it! What a good life he'd have, given a reasonable share of luck.

After a jubilant lap of honor, the group assembled around Ricky in the middle of the ground. He raised his baseball hat, slicked back his hair, repositioned the cap and then started on what I thought would be a euphoric recap of game and season. But, no, what followed was this:

"OK, guys. Be back here at six tonight and we'll do pizzas and drinks. Enjoy the wine but don't do anything silly. If you're at drinking age, don't get paralytic, and don't drive if you've had a few too many. The guys under drinking age can have a beer so long as their parents write a note giving permission. But only one. Friends and family are welcome and we'll finish around nine."

And then they adjourned to the change rooms.

On the way home the contented, mud-encrusted fourteen-year-old accepted plaudits with grace, unplugging his iPod to receive each new commendation and to call his elderly grandmother.

After we'd recapped the game and Elli had explained some of the innumerable technicalities we'd missed, I said: "I was surprised that Ricky didn't rave about the performance out on the field. Did he say much about the game afterward in the rooms?"

"No," said Elli, "he didn't say much. He mainly cracked jokes and reminded us to leave our club gear in the rooms. Stuff like that. And just in case you're wondering, Dad, he didn't say anything about fitness."

"Oh."

"Actually," said the boy, "the main thing he said to me was: 'Elliot, make sure you nail plenty of pizza tonight, because the bigger you are, the harder they fall.'"

Five

The "logic" of life-changing "choices"

And thus the native hue of resolution
Is sicklied o'er with the pale cast of thought

—Shakespeare, *Hamlet*

By intellect and art I here have brought thee;
Take thine own pleasure for thy guide henceforth;
Beyond the steep ways and the narrow art thou.
Behold the sun, that shines upon thy forehead;
Behold the grass, the flowerets, and the shrubs
Which of itself alone this land produces.
Until rejoicing come the beauteous eyes
Which weeping caused me to come unto thee,
Thou canst sit down, and thou canst walk among
    them.
Expect no more or word or sign from me;
Free and upright and sound is thy free-will,
And error were it not to do its bidding;
Thee o'er thyself I therefore crown and mitre!

—Virgil's last words to Dante in *The Divine Comedy*

... the Sea Hag was relaxing on a green couch:
"How pleasant
To spend one's vacation *en la casa de Popeye*," she
scratched
Her cleft chin's solitary hair. She remembered
spinach

—John Ashbery, "Farm Implements and
Rutabagas in a Landscape"

A s a fourteen-year-old I was angry, defiant and furious at the constraints of my conventional, recently established Church of England school for boys, modeled on the traditional English public school. I had started there a couple of years prior when my family moved from metropolitan Melbourne to Mount Eliza, a coastal town, then small and rustic, thirty miles from the city.

I was flamboyant with friends, often depressed, humiliatingly shy with girls and flying in all directions toward absurdly unrealistic ambitions—playing league football, being an Australian Picasso. One lunchtime, playing kick-to-kick on one of the school ovals, the first of these dreams disintegrated. I'd flown for a mark, seemingly best positioned in a pack to pluck the ball from the air, when I heard a firm *thwack* as it lodged in another pair of hands. Star athlete, Ross Johnson, who would go on to play league football, had better assessed the flight of the ball and, with the aid of superior height and a well-timed jump, had snatched it just above my outstretched hands. He nonchalantly touched down and launched a perfectly spinning drop punt from three paces that scythed the misty winter air and flew further than I could possibly kick. At that moment, I knew deep down, without yet quite admitting it to myself, that I would never be a league footballer, no matter how hard I tried.

It was a slightly puzzling fact of school life that our art teacher was also the Master of the school military cadets. With good reason I despised the latter activity—a Pythonesque compulsory exercise in mindless compliance—and decided to throw the teacher into a state of confusion by going AWOL from cadet exercises and letting myself into the art room to work on my paintings. What was he to do? Punish my dereliction of military duty when I was using the time to exercise the creativity he tried in his kindly, if limited, way to foster? In fact, as an art teacher he was *too* kind, because I had as much chance of being a professional painter as I had of being a professional footballer.

The campaign I launched to have myself demobbed from the cadets took time, partly, I suppose, because the art teacher felt obliged to go easy on my creative AWOLs. Eventually, though, I achieved the desired outcome with a friend who shared my contempt for knuckle-headed conformity. With a wheelbarrow full of pinecones we ambushed our own regiment during an exercise in bushland beside the school. But even this didn't move the art teacher to fury. As I look back on the brat I was then, one of the more painful memories is of the kindly way he broke what he must have imagined to be painful news: "Richard, I'm very sorry to tell you this, but I'm afraid we're going to have to ask you to hand in your kit bag."

When I heard recently that this decent man had died, I was sorry to hear it, in more ways than one.

I'm amazed now at how brazen I was in those days. An old school friend, Peter Monk, recently recalled an incident I seem completely to have repressed: during a class with a rather ineffectual teacher who was struggling to maintain control I apparently let myself out of an open window into the flowerbed below, climbed back in with a flower in hand and proceeded to chew on it. Though I was already interested in modern literature, I doubt that I had then heard of the occasion on which the poet Ezra Pound, unenthused by a disquisition by fellow poet, W. B. Yeats, ate a bowl of tulips that adorned the table at which he was sitting during Yeats' address. In any case, according to Peter what I chomped on was a shasta daisy.

In that world even a troubled, introspective, nascently intellectual kid could get by well enough with his peers if he was funny, loud, better than average at sport, apparently fearless and good at his studies. My general demeanor among friends suggested that I could "call spirits from the vasty deep" of nearby Port Phillip Bay, and perhaps only a few of the more independent-minded among my cohort might have bothered to inquire whether such aquatic visitants had, in fact, turned up.

It was at about this time, when certain teachers were muttering the *s* word—suspension—despite my scholarly dedication, that a new teacher appeared during recess in the school courtyard. His fine, straight, jet-black hair was swept back, his black goatee carefully trimmed. He was dapperly attired in sports coat, slacks, formal shirt and tie, and had about him a solicitousness edged with unease. He walked up to me and my friend Oliver Hopkins, smiling warmly, and seemed genuinely eager to make contact—human contact, we felt, not the more generic sort that a newly arrived teacher might routinely initiate. What really struck me, though, were his intense dark brown eyes. I said to Oliver later that the man had "burning eyes." They were the eyes of someone unusually alive and alive in unusual ways. This was Dr. Ian Guthridge, or "Guthers" as we affectionately came to call him.

We soon learned that he had just left the Jesuit Order after twenty years. Since he'd taught school during some of those years he wasn't new to teaching, but many other aspects of what we'd think of as normal life were basically foreign to him. Whose eyes wouldn't burn amid such a life transition? He'd studied philosophy at the University of Melbourne, had done a PhD in theology in Rome and was, among other things, a good athlete and a lover of the arts, insofar as the Order had allowed him to indulge such passions. He had traveled widely and lived in the US, and now here he was. He had left the Order penniless and gravitated to this area because the position of Senior History Master was vacant and because his mother lived nearby.

He was a man of ideas who had departed the priesthood after a long and anguished battle with religious doubt and disaffection with the coercive "cocoon-like" quality of monastic life. His slightly edgy energy and blazing eyes were those of a deeply questioning man on an intellectual and spiritual journey. For me and other non-conforming boys, the opportunity to speak uninhibitedly with this dynamic spirit from a world we could barely imagine was thrilling—almost a liberation (though, to be fair, there were other teachers whose conversation we enjoyed too). We could talk to him about religion and the meaning of life; about history, the ambiguities of literature, art, the Continent, the US, and much else. I don't think I was any closer to Guthers than several of the other students, but he became a significant figure for me at an unsettled and impressionable time, partly because he offered a sort of empathic but low-key guidance. Like all good teachers he was inclined "To give full growth to that which still doth grow." But there was another, more intangible aspect to it: being around him, seeing how he questioned, moved, responded, his way of being in the world, what he found funny or absurd, provided a welcome opportunity for emulation. I felt intuitively that following his lead could help me figure out who I might be, and help me become that person.

Perhaps six months after Guthridge's arrival, our mercurial, stern but not wholly unimaginative clergyman-headmaster called me in for what I assumed would be another disciplinary interview. To my astonishment he told me that I had been selected to be a School Prefect the next year. Me, the daisy-chewing, pine-cone-hurling scourge of the staffroom! I learnt much later that this was Ian Guthridge's suggestion and that it had struck one of the less frozen chords in the headmaster's wintry but unpredictable personality.

It was a strikingly astute and empathic idea on Guthridge's part. A rebel who had departed a religious order, he could see in me a kindred spirit, albeit one more than twenty years his junior. But I think he also sensed that this apparently defiant young man actually craved success and laudation, and would be more than happy to receive them on thoroughly conventional terms. And what could be more conventional than the office of School Prefect, entrusted to students who would exercise leadership strictly according to the ethos of school status quo?

Guthridge had seen a split in me between defiant individualism and biddable conformity, a fissure that remained, not least in my working life. I've seen it, too, in many academic colleagues who have devoted their intellectual lives to radical social critique and yet have been so ambitious for conventional affirmation that perceived professional setbacks—failed job or promotions applications, hostile book reviews—have hit them with the force of a psychological crisis. Indeed, this split condition is, as the French sociologist Émile Durkheim observed over a century ago, a very common phenomenon in modern Western society where the individual, no longer so clearly defined by class, religion, and other traditional markers of identity, must do a lot of identity-work—fashioning his or her identity through achievement and other means—in order to gain the feeling of viable selfhood. It's an aspect of what, in his book on suicide, Durkheim called "anomie."

Thus, I was far more chuffed by the headmaster's news than I was going to let on, and when I announced it coyly to my intellectually progressive, but also status-craving Jewish mother, Fleur, I knew I could depend on a delighted reaction: "We'd better go out and buy some new school shirts so that I can smarten up a bit."

"Why, dear?"

"Oh. I'll be a School Prefect next year."

"Oh, that's *wonderful*, dear!"

And, just for a moment, our contempt for the more starchy and churchy aspects of the school evaporated.

The boy on whom Ian Guthridge made such an impression had, quite fortuitously and serendipitously, been prepared for that encounter by his own personal history.

My father, Paul, was a sad casualty of anomie: an acculturated Jew and prone to depression, he had over-invested in the Career as the High Road to personal identity and validation. Being under-confident, though highly ambitious, he had passed up golden opportunities like a scholarship to Harvard, and had set me, quite unconsciously at first, on a lifelong search for self-assured and wise mentor figures. But of course I did inevitably model myself on this good, accomplished, and intellectual man. I gained a great deal from him, but I also inherited his tendency to depression, absorbed his habit of self-doubt, and became, like him, far too dependent on professional success as a source of self-definition and self-esteem.

If I was going to flourish and overcome these aspects of his legacy, I would need to draw upon the example of more confident, buoyant people endowed with toughness and strategic nous. One such was Zelman Cowen, my father's closest friend and one of the most successful Australian men of his generation. Conversations with Zelman were fun and stimulating, and I was fascinated by the way, as I would put it now, his identity synthesized acculturated Jewish intellectuality and conventional public success as it was understood in his—our—adoptive anglicized culture.

Growing up, I met a lot of intellectual Jews, many of them intense, pretty confident, but not really fiery or defiant. They too had been anglicized, and for very good reason they felt deeply indebted to the security of post-pogrom and post-Holocaust Australia. So they weren't, on the whole, what you would call rebels. But somewhere in among all of this I became aware of figures who went by names like "the American Jewish intellectual," and "the New York Jewish writers." I was lucky to grow up in an environment in which such things were in the air despite our geographical isolation.

In the bookshelves at home I found two of Saul Bellow's novels, including *Herzog*. Herzog, a deracinated middle-aged American Jewish intellectual in meltdown after the crack-up of his second marriage, is writhing under "the bone-breaking burden of selfhood." He writes blazing letters to intellectual giants, friends and others, which he never posts. By the time I got to the calmer waters of the novel's later chapters I had been mesmerized by the man's unruly, explosive brilliance, a version of what Charlotte Brontë's Rochester calls "paving hell with energy." I was able to learn more about Bellow and co, from my parents, from

Zelman, who had lived and worked among such people in the US, and from a woman by the name of Margaret Falkiner, a charismatic and highly accomplished American southerner who had moved to Australia with her children to marry an Australian naval officer. I met her, late in my school years, because I had become besotted with her middle daughter, Elizabeth. When I talked to Margaret about possibly going to university in America, she dismissed with a wave of an imperious arm the conventional wisdom in Australia in those days that you could not do your undergraduate degree in the US. The sanctioned path was to do an Honors degree here and then do another undergraduate degree at Oxford or Cambridge. It was Margaret who showed me how to apply for undergraduate scholarships to American colleges and universities and who told me about the Wien International Scholarship Program at Brandeis, a predominantly Jewish university near Boston.

I was far too anxious and obsessed by the need to do brilliantly to do really well in the state matriculation exams at the end of high school, but I think Guthridge and a couple of other sympathetic teachers wrote enthusiastically of my excellent school results and my intellectual promise. Armed with a piece of well-crafted autobiographical salesmanship—the first of my many adventures in autobiographical life writing—I successfully applied for a Wien Scholarship. I took it with relish, despite my parents' misgivings about how I would fare emotionally, the marketability of an American undergraduate degree, and my mother's fear that she was being displaced in my affections by my girlfriend and her imposingly self-assured mother.

When I arrived at the attractive hilly residential campus of Brandeis University in Waltham, a suburb about twenty minutes from Boston, one of the first things I encountered was a legend. Allen Grossman was said to be the most inspiring, charismatic and unusual teacher there. He was also apparently highly eccentric and I wondered what part this might play in his popularity.

I enrolled in what was to become his famous Humanities I course, whose vast two-semester syllabus ran from Homer to the twentieth century, and turned up for the first lecture.

The man who shuffled up to the podium moved as though his brain had to send prompts to his limbs via satellite. He really did have the aura of an absent-minded professor. His receding straight brown hair dangled over his shirt collar and he had incongruous ear-long sideburns. He was wearing what I soon learned was his customary campus garb: faded white shirt, bow tie, a passably smart but loose-hanging patterned sports coat, a subdued but ill-assorted vest, nondescript slacks, and Dunlop Volley tennis shoes. Dottings of stubble suggested that he might be a more dab hand with a typewriter than a razor, and he seemed to chew and suck incessantly upon a bulbous pipe with a long black stem.

But what struck me most about his face were his eyes. You might expect a man of such turbulent and intense energy to have fiery eyes, but his were nothing of the sort. Light blue with an almond tinge, they looked sedate, a touch withdrawn, and always tired, encircled by light gray-ish rings. At first I took this as a sign of overwork, and this was no doubt partly so; but I came to see that these were the eyes of a man so deeply immersed in books and the world of the imagination that he lived a borderless life between them and the everyday world. I sensed this was another way of being in the world—a bit Herzog-like—and I found it immensely compelling.

Legend had it that after the collapse of his first marriage Grossman had suffered such a severe breakdown that for a time he lost the power of speech. I assume this was a yarn spun to account for his unusual speech mannerisms. Though a man of rich and powerful intellect, his speech and academic writing, and even some of his otherworldly-but-earthy poetry, lacked a certain fluency. He tended to talk in bursts that seemed strung together with varying degrees of adeptness. If, as was quite often the case, he was wanting to convey a rather Delphic abstraction, the idea might come out in a lecture or seminar like this: "The lyric moves from … least … differentiation of the self (the opening) … toward most differentiation of the self (at the close), from the dark embrace before the lark … to the full day of cognitive self-recognition."

Despite the forbidding air of mystery, you felt that you might well get the point once you'd looked up the lark reference, or asked someone what it meant. Similarly, many of what were to become his legendary academic formulations had a trademark clunkiness, like his passion-ately held belief that poetry was a vast trans-historical act of creative spiritual labor, an almost magical "principle of power invoked by all of us against our vanishing"—that is, against the annulling powers of death and the forgetting that consigns most lives to oblivion.

I have occasionally mused on how Grossman would fare on one of the teacher assessment questionnaires with which university students are inundated nowadays:

1. On a scale of 1–10, how much new information did you acquire from the lectures?

    Answer: Hard to say, but maybe 5

2. On a scale from 1–10, how clearly were the ideas in the lectures explained?

    Answer: Well, if you mean *clearly*—2

3. On a scale of 1–10, how highly would you rate the lecturer?

    Answer: 10

    Please add any further comment you might like to make.

    Most of the course went right over my head but it didn't matter. I came out of the lectures dying to know what he was on about, to read and talk until I got it. The guy made me fall in love with ideas, with books. I loved his passion, his weirdness.

Fortunately another of Grossman's several tones was more immediately accessible to beginners like me. An example that has stayed with me was his comment during a class that [Robert] "Frost was a strategic son of a bitch." He wasn't referring so much to recent biographical revelations of the calculating man behind Frost's artfully constructed public image as a plainspoken "woodsy" bard, but rather to the fact that many of those beautifully haunting rustic poems are exquisitely disguised syllogisms:

> And sorry I could not travel both
> And be one traveler, long I stood
> And looked down one as far as I could
> To where it bent beneath the undergrowth;
> Then took the other, as just as fair,
> And having perhaps the better claim,
> Because it was grassy and wanted wear

Grossman's verbal mannerisms included a sonorous "Ya, ya, ya," when agreeing (or pretending to agree) with a point made during discussion, and a laugh a couple of octaves higher, which went, roughly, "Yak-yak-yak." For a man so serious he laughed with surprising ease.

The crack-up legend (if that's what it was) was further fuelled by a volume of his poems that several of us acolytes purchased at the university bookshop. Re-reading *The Recluse* now I'm surprised by how beautiful and even mellifluous some of the poems are, but there remains still the sense of a soul in pieces laboriously re-assembling itself, as if from traumatized memory:

> And I am paralyzed with loneliness
> And cannot think except to cry aloud
> Holds the wide world any slim and glittering
>   thing

> For which my heart's need has not a use and
> gratefulness.

Even now as a retired academic I don't really know how to characterize Allen Grossman's mind. This is not just because he was so much more learned than I could ever be, but also because he was in many respects a one-off. I'd hazard that he was a combination of High Romantic poet and critic, ecumenical Jewish mystic, and cultural proselytizer fired by a powerful sense that the world needed redeeming and might yet be redeemed, and that redemption could not occur without the transformative and creative energies of the educated imagination.

So where did the vernacular—the "son of a bitch" tone – fit in all of this? From a lower-middle-class Minnesotan Jewish family (his father owned a car yard) Grossman had an earthy side. His poetry can swerve wonderfully, sometimes disorientingly, from vatic to the vernacular. A fine poem in his volume *Descartes' Loneliness* speaks of Descartes' search for a final "ground" or guarantee of the conviction that "I exist." The poem ends:

>   ... For
> after a most careful search, I have been
> unable to discover the *ground* of that
> conviction—unless it be imagined a lonely
> workman on a dizzy scaffold unfolds
> a sign at evening and puts his mark to it.

The image—of a worker high up on a construction scaffold demonstrating to those below what the absolute guarantee of one's existence might look like—is vintage

Grossman. The construction scaffold becomes the site, in both senses, of dizzying revelation.

I was earthy myself, but I could not access that fundamental aspect of my personality in Grossman's company. By contrast, my friend Alan Shapiro, another Grossman protégé and now one of America's finest poets, had no such problem. Alan, who had come to Brandeis on a basketball scholarship and was himself from a lower-middle-class Jewish background, could gag around with Grossman and have him "Yak-yak-yakking" over the jumbo-sized Cokes the great man swilled from plastic tumblers in the student cafeteria.

I've sometimes wondered why I was all stumbling unease with Grossman, as I have been with other eminent academics whose powers I was greatly impressed by. A Freudian might suggest that I secretly desired their crowns and was gummed up by a sort of guilt at harboring ruthless aspirations. But I don't think this was it. The people in question generally saw real promise in me, but I lived in fear that on account of my limited scholarly equipment—my slow reading and poor memory—I could not fulfill their expectations which so closely mirrored my most cherished hopes. So I kept myself under wraps with them without wanting to. This was a continual source of frustration because I craved the sort of mentor-friendship that would relax and reassure me into enjoying what, after all, I very much wanted to do.

Still, I managed to indicate to Grossman that I was thinking about an academic career in literary studies. A sensitive man, he clearly registered my insecurity because he took pains to make clear that he regarded this as a serious matter.

Another of his unusual mannerisms involved referring to us students with striking formality as Mr., Ms., Miss. This was odd in a university that had been radicalized in opposition to the Vietnam War and whose staff list boasted a good many rough-mannered Jews. But it wasn't pomposity on his part, much less the pulling of rank. What he meant to convey by such formality was that in reading, thinking, writing, and conversing, we were about serious Socratic business. We weren't just kids undergoing a formal education. We were *thinkers* whom he took seriously and who had every right to take themselves seriously as well.

During a class late in my first year, Grossman suggested I pop by his office later that day. The office, as I recall, was dimly lit with a circular table in the middle to facilitate conversation, and it absolutely reeked of tobacco smoke. Like his desk, the table was strewn with books and papers. The office's welcoming den-like intimacy went some way toward putting me at my ease.

"Mr. Freadman," he commenced, "I have noted your interest in perhaps becoming an academic in this field."

"Yes," I said, and then something to the effect of, "and your classes have played quite an important part in this."

"Ya, ya, ya. This is good. Ya, ya. I can see that you have been much engaged. You have been working hard. If you decide on this course of action, I think you can do well, but you will need to read everything for three years."

This was the moment that clinched the deal, that convinced me to become an academic. I bounced out of that office as the Woody Allen figure, Micky, floats out of the doctor's surgery and waltzes down the street in *Hannah and Her Sisters* after getting the all-clear on an ominous x-ray. Just as his euphoria soon dissipates at the recognition that one day a medical test *will* bring bad news, so later, as I pondered Grossman's rather mysterious three-year time frame, I wondered apprehensively what "everything" might include and, still more anxiously, how much a slow reader like me could get through in such a time.

But the worry didn't dampen my ardor for long; it hovered in the background, a shadow of self-doubt, as I set my will to becoming not perhaps like Grossman—he was inimitable and unique—but the sort of academic and intellectual he might approve of and the sort of person he had helped me to think I wanted to be.

⁂

So what actually goes on when one makes life-changing "choices" such as I have just described?

Hamlet is perhaps Western culture's most famous and penetrating account of fraught decision-making. Late in his "To be or not to be" soliloquy, Hamlet says of his current state:

> And thus the native hue of resolution
> Is sicklied o'er with the pale cast of thought

This suggestion that there can be a sort of "gut" or visceral certainty in decision-making which "thought" can only impede is too simple; the play as a whole shows that the situation and the state in which Hamlet feels that he must make decisions is made up of many mutually influencing strands—circumstantial, psychosexual, ethical, cultural, and so on—and that tragedy springs in part from a warped relationship between "resolution" and "thought" that occurs, as Horatio says at the end, "while men's minds are wild." We have a clunky but useful term nowadays for the idea that various and often interacting causes bring something about: we say the process is multifactorial. Freud, who was of course fascinated by *Hamlet*, coined the term "overdetermination" to express the idea of multiple causes, all of which are essential to the outcome in which they issue. But even a Proust or a Shakespeare, or theorists of things like decision-making, chaos, and motivation, cannot capture anything like the full complexity of patterns such as these.

Yet autobiography, memoir and related genres exist partly in order to make the best sense possible of how the autobiographer came to be who he or she is, and this process of review generally includes tracking major "choices" made along the way. Regardless of whether or not the life or the career in question has been exceptional, such narrative reflection, if practiced with honesty and discernment, has intrinsic value. There has been nothing exceptional about my life or career, but I find tracing the "logic" of my important "choices" essential to my attempt in late middle age to make sense of my life.

Here's a very condensed sketch. Certain bedrock facts or "initial conditions," as chaos theorists call them, "set the scene" for my life: being born an Australian Jew of reflective parents and coming into the world with a certain genetically given set of personal characteristics. Some of these factors give rise to fairly predictable outcomes, for instance, that being Jewish will play a significant part in the way I try to establish my own identity, and the fact that my parents are the sort of people who would have *Herzog* on their shelves. Then there are patterns of emulation—I model on my mother's unconventionality and my father's intellectual rigor, for instance—but also patterns of differentiation associated with these identifications. I feel that I need to defuse some powerful sources of identification in order to become "me"; so I wrest greater emotional distance from my intense and feminizing mother, and determine to live with greater decisiveness than my father who seems to have made a mess of some of his major life decisions. The feeling of feminization and paternal disappointment both fuel anger, but this too would arise from many causes, not least the characteristic tumult of adolescence itself. Anger, intellectual fire and a propensity for risk-taking then receive impetus and also direction, a sense of purpose, from the lightning rod figure of Ian Guthridge. Such figures don't miraculously transform one's life, as in a conversion, but rather attract and recombine already-influential factors, providing revised, clearer and more compelling images of what life might be, and more focus for aspirational energies.

Now more layers of serendipity cut in. I happen to fall in love with an American girl, socially confident enough to release me from my shyness with women, who intends returning to the US. This powerful new condition then interacts with other causal sequences already in motion: the fact I am a possessive, sometimes apocalyptic, lover who cannot stand to contemplate separation from his girlfriend is probably in part a consequence of my relationship with my mother.

Certain factors seem to group as well as converge, so that particular themes and symbols take on special and influential importance in my psychic landscape. With so many important paths leading, alone and in combination, in this direction, it is hardly surprising that important ones coalesce around "America." America takes on such psychological significance—becomes a symbolic lightning rod – that, metaphorically speaking, it can pump new energies back into the causal system, augmenting, neutralizing, or transforming existing ones. It's at about this point in the process that I "make" my "decision"; and then, "as way leads onto way," in Frost's words, comes Grossman, another lightning rod figure, and the career decision.

Chaos theory predicates that systems combine aspects of both predictability and randomness and, insofar as a personal narrative can be seen as a "system," this might well hold, to some extent at least, for the narrative structures of our lives where, as nuanced psychological analysis often shows, specifiable initial conditions can lead to unpredictable outcomes.

Beneath all of this lies another level of complexity best described as one's existential orientation. Sartre argued that particular choices we make, muddle, or refuse can only be understood against the background of a prior choice we have already and unconsciously made: the choice to be the sort of person who takes chances and risks, or the kind who does not. My father was talented and ambitious, but deep down he seemed programmed not to take his chances.

What I've traced above is, of course, a snapshot. Given reasonable neurological health, the whole pattern will roll on, variously mediated at different stages of life, until death. To ask why I came to specialize in and to write autobiography instead of doing work more like, say, Allen Grossman's would be a later installment of the story, but I suspect that some of the mechanisms I've described would be very much in evidence there too.

∞

Ben

In my early thirties I had the good fortune to acquire my stepson, Ben. My fortune back then was certainly better than his because I lacked the maturity needed to step-parent well and was often distracted and irritable as I tried to wind up what seemed like an interminable PhD and start my university teaching career at the same time. It was just as well for Ben that he moved between the two parental homes for quite a while, because it gave him breaks from me and time with his more easygoing father. They say kids can be lucky with their parents, but parents can be lucky with their kids too: Ben, now thirty-seven, cut me a lot of slack until I could get my act together. No doubt it's harder for stepchildren to make demands than it is for biological ones, but Ben just is an accepting and sympathetic guy anyway.

At six foot four he is big, almost brawny, and solid. But his slightly splayed-footed gait and ambling mode of locomotion bespeak a gentle man. His broad face and light blue eyes can modulate rapidly from fun to brooding seriousness, but if his confidence remains a bit in arrears of his talents and virtues, he knows how not to sweat the small stuff and to have fun. He's a people person with a gift for friendship, and a marvelous sibling to my two "biological" kids.

They are amused when, one evening after a weekend family meal, iPhone set on Voice Memos, I draw him aside and start plying him with questions about Chaos Theory. I've become interested in what it seems to offer our understanding of the role of causation and chance in the way human lives unfold, and this young man with a Psychology degree and an MBA, despite having an extremely busy corporate job, seems to read everything.

I explain why I'm interested, and he says: "Yeah, you can see it in the life of organizations too, not just individuals."

"Say more."

"Well, basically the idea is that you have initiating conditions for something, say the weather, which is where this idea came from. Weather patterns. Meteorology. If you know the *exact* initiating conditions, you can predict how some things will behave for a while, but then other, unpredictable causal factors cut in and change its course. And those factors can have huge, *gigantic* ramifications: two small storm systems happening to collide in one part of the globe might cause a hundred thousand deaths in some other distant part; a toxic CEO who is already wrecking morale in a business can cause a meltdown if financial markets crash unpredictably; a woman who starts life with a good childhood and temperament can suffer major mental illness if some maniac comes from nowhere and rapes her."

"So, if you take the weather deaths," I say, "it means that you can't predict what will happen once you get further out in time or further out geographically?"

"Yep. That's what's called the Butterfly Effect in Chaos Theory. The idea is that a butterfly flapping its wings here might cause something—maybe something major—to happen way out in the system."

"So, on this view there is a system?"

"To a degree. If you mean that a system is something in which laws operate, then I guess so. But if you mean that systems have the property of predictability, then, no. On this view, predictability can only go so far, until things are blown off course. And even the initiating conditions don't make stuff entirely predictable except for a very short distance out because it turns out that there will be differences between initiating conditions that are so minuscule that we can't empirically measure them, but they will cause huge variation further up the line."

And then he tells me about an experiment where balls of apparently exactly the same size, attached to cords of apparently exactly the same length, are released pendulum-wise at ostensibly exactly the same speed, from what is measured to be exactly the same place, and yet the arcs they trace assume strikingly different shapes.

"OK," I say, "what about people?"

"With people it's infinitely more complicated, because how could you claim to know all the initiating circumstances of someone's life? Even identical twins turn out different. Maybe one has a slightly different birth experience; then at school maybe they're put in different classes and make some different friends; they marry different women. So the start is microscopically different and other factors cut in to make it macroscopic."

"I see why some psychologists are interested in it."

"It sounds very relevant to what you're doing. All your stuff about people's life stories, actually. But, in a way, Chaos Theory tells you something you already know, which is that the more information you have, the more predictable things are. It's just that there are huge practical limits to how much information we can have and where knowledge fuzzes out."

"It's a kind of ideal modeling," I say, "like climate modeling?"

"Yeah, there's something very Platonic about it, though you have to have theories. But there are theories and theories. Try running an organization on a theory that doesn't take the individual psychology of those individuals who make it into consideration. That's why so many companies go down the toilet and why so many people are unhappy at work. Ideally every manager should invite each employee to write a sort of mini-autobiography they can read."

—◆◆◆—

I saw Allen Grossman once or twice when I called in at Brandeis over the years, but otherwise lost touch with him. I had the feeling he'd become a bit puzzled by my lack of self-confidence and a bit disappointed at the tinny, achievement-for-its-own-sake side of my ambition. But this may be a projection on my part. Emulation figures retain a strange authority throughout life. And, anyway, some of his colossal ambition may have been a bit tinny too. He wasn't a god.

I followed his career and knew that he'd eventually moved to another university and had gained a fine national reputation as teacher, poet and scholar. When he died of Alzheimer's Disease in 2014—*Alzheimer's, of all things!*—there were fine obituaries and sad but deeply appreciative emails passed between some of his former students.

From the best teachers we learn much more than mere subject matter. I've always loved (while sometimes fearing) being around them, close up, because then you can see what an adult life infused with commitments, passions, and attitudes looks like and how this might help you to fashion an authentic life of your own. I sometimes wonder how many first-year Australian university students get such opportunities now: staff cuts mean that much of their teaching is done by postgraduates and they access many of their lectures online. Humor's a huge part of what you see close up: not scripted quips in lectures, good though they are, but rather how experienced, reflective people's sense of the absurd expresses ways of living, of dealing with pain, incongruity, tragedy, and, of course, mortality—what Proust calls "the general law of oblivion" and Grossman, "our vanishing."

Though I couldn't horse about with Allen Grossman the way Alan Shapiro could, it was obvious that Grossman too was a very funny man. One of my favorite memories of him comes from a lecture in which he read aloud a sublimely absurd poem by John Ashbery called "Farm Implements and Rutabagas in a Landscape", which features Popeye in a state of obscure chagrin ("Popeye sits in thunder"). Most of the familiar Popeye cast are enveloped in the drama: the Sea Hag, who scratches "her cleft chin's solitary hair"; Wimpy who "scratched / The part of his head under his hat"; Swee'pea, a note attached to his bib warning that "'Thunder / And tears are unavailing'". Olive's advent is dramatic: "Olive came hurtling through the window; its geraniums scratched / Her long thigh …"After some High Romantic phasing ("At his own astonished becoming") thunder again prevails: "domestic thunder / The color of spinach." But Popeye's part in all of this remains opaque to the end: "Popeye chuckled and scratched / His balls: it sure was pleasant to spend a day in the country."

During the forty-five or so years since I'd last seen Ian Guthridge I'd heard occasional word of him: his innovative career in adult education, his books on issues ranging from religion and spirituality, to women's biography, the arts, and his contributions to discussion of social issues.

A few months ago I saw him and his second wife, Elaine, at a wine bar near where they live in Middle Park. He was waiting for me at an outdoor table, his hair just a touch thinner and now white but still swept back, his skin a little patchier. Otherwise, though, this man of eighty-five was pretty much as I had remembered him: the old edgy, complex energy—and those blazing eyes as intense as ever.

I'd heard that he'd written a memoir about his entry into the priesthood, his life there and his decision to leave it. At my request he'd brought a copy along with him. We seemed to pick up where we'd left off so many years ago. He told me he now considers his essential orientation to be existential, but still in some sense religious. He said that he'd had to write three versions of his memoir, *Give Me a Child When He Is Young ...*, the title of which is drawn from a claim reputedly made by Saint Ignatius of Loyola, founder of the Jesuit Order: "Give me a child when he is young and I will mold the man." The first version was too angry for public consumption, the second too anodyne in over-correction, the third, he hoped, more balanced.

In the book, he reveals that he, too, was an angry and rebellious schoolboy, and takes the reader inside the mind of the troubled ex-priest who landed in a schoolyard in Mount Eliza feeling "I had never lived at all." He writes sympathetically of the non-conformist group of boys who didn't want to be in the cadets, or didn't want to play sport, and of how he designed classes that would open out the complexities of the individual's relationship to the society around him. In his self-portrait of a searching, intense, conflicted, competitive man excited by life's possibilities, and fuming at their needless institutional thwarting, I could see many of my own traits. No wonder we hit it off.

The book is, among other things, a chronicle of his major life choices: the complex factors (including his inadequate relationship with his father) that led to his choice of a religious vocation; the way that mounting but strangely intermittent doubt and anger caused him to leave. Remarkably he writes: "Ordination day was the unhappiest day of my life," and yet it took him another fifteen years to decide to depart the Order.

One of his many striking metaphors describes his state of mind as he approaches Ordination Day, torn between commitment, doubt, aspirational energy and depression: "My mind was like a sky filled with clouds at different levels—all going in different directions at the same time: do this, do that, do something else."

Little wonder he got the decision wrong, if indeed he did.

Six

The challenged reader who mistook himself for a man of letters

—shall I go on?—No.

> —Laurence Sterne, *Tristram Shandy*

There somewhere man is too, vast conglomerate of all of nature's kingdoms, as lonely and as bound. And in that block the prey is lodged and thinks himself a being apart.

> —Samuel Beckett, *Molloy*

How is one to decide whether an inborn affliction will paralyse or galvanize?

> —Arthur Koestler, *The Sleepwalkers*

A piece of Sterne's *The Life and Opinions of Tristram Shandy, Gentleman* can look like this:

——Lord have mercy upon me, said my father
to himself— o   o   o   o   o   o   o   o   o
o   o   o   o   o   o   o   o   o   o   o   o

o   o   o   o   o   o   o   o   o   o   o   o

Or like this description of *Le Fever,* a dangerously ill
friend of Tristram's Uncle Toby:

———The blood and spirits of *Le Fever,* which
were waxing cold and slow within him, and were
retreating to their last citadel, the heart,———
rallied back,———the film forsook his eyes for
a moment,———he looked up wishfully in my
uncle *Toby's* face,———then cast a look upon his
boy,———and that *lingament,* fine as it was,———
was never broken———

Nature instantly ebb'd again,———the film
returned to its place,———the pulse fluttered,———
stopp'd———went   on———throb'd———stopp'd
again———moved———stopp'd———shall I go
on?———No.

The book is a spoof-autobiography-cum-spoof-novel
written in the eighteenth century as the modern novel and
the modern confessional autobiography were on the rise.

After the first twenty-four pages (in my edition) you
suddenly slam into a wall:

The black page, which was pitch-black in the editions printed during Sterne's lifetime, represents the tombstone of Tristram's (not Shakespeare's) *Yorick*, the clergyman who, though already dead at the beginning, is, by way of Sterne's chronological zigzags, accorded the honor of uttering the book's last words, almost five hundred pages later. The story ends with the news that Tristram's father, Walter's, prized bull is sterile. When Tristram's simple mother asks what the men's double entendre-riddled conversation concerning the bull is all about, *Yorick*, a cock 'n' bull artist if ever there was one, replies in terms that apply equally to the bull and to the book itself:

> A COCK and a BULL, said *Yorick*——And one
> of the best of its kind, I ever heard.

On the reverse side of the black page is another just like it, the idea here apparently being that it provides a blank slate on which the reader may imagine another of the novel's characters, Widow Wadman. This apparent freedom to do as you like as you read, rather as Tristram seems to do as he writes, is one aspect of the book's dizzying reading experience.

Perhaps we don't so much slam into these walls as clatter or stumble. "Slam" would imply having a good deal of speed up, but the text's freakish and digressive structural rhythms—"Digressions," Tristram tells us, "incontestably, are the sunshine;——they are the life, the soul of reading"; his narrative "is digressive, and it is progressive too"—slows reading down, making what comes easily to efficient readers quite difficult, albeit hilarious.

Tristram Shandy doesn't let you "get lost in the book" in the usual way: to get lost in it generally means losing your place, being disoriented, not, as we colloquially use the term, to float through the book as if it were an extension of our customary reality or an equally habitable alternative one. Tristram has a good deal to say about words themselves, reveling in them even while cautioning against their obscurantist tendencies, their formidable *look* on the page:

> I hate set dissertations,——and above all things in the world, 'tis one of the silliest things in one of them, to darken your hypothesis by placing a number of tall, opake words, one before another, in a right line, betwixt your own and your reader's conception,——when in all likelihood, if you had looked about, you might have seen something standing, or hanging up, which would have cleared the point at once——"for what hindrance, hurt, or harm doth the laudable desire of knowledge bring to any man, if even from a sot, a pot, a fool, a stool, a winter-mittain, a truckle for a pully, the lid of a goldsmith's crucible, an oyl bottle, an old slipper, or a cane chair?"

In making reading hard, the black marks on the page a touch "opake," it merely magnifies the experience of reading as I have always known it.

———※———

I had joined my mother, Fleur, and a friend of hers at the kitchen table when I was perhaps eight or nine. Sickly health—an underactive immune system, bronchitis, asthma, pneumonia, sinus infections—kept me at home a lot during childhood, and so I'd often meet friends who dropped in to see Fleur. I gathered from her that this particular friend was a librarian, an emissary from the world of books so highly prized in my middle-class Jewish world. My recollection is that I was reading an illustrated children's guide to human anatomy.

Some already-nagging need in me, like David Copperfield's "old unhappy feeling," was momentarily appeased when the friend congratulated me on the difficulty of the material I was reading. Craving still more affirmation, I opened the book at the table while she and my mother chatted over tea. If memory serves—and mine often doesn't – I was reading about Harvey and the nature of the blood. Whatever it was, I was sufficiently engrossed to drift briefly into that zone where the world contracts to just you and the book, and anything else, if heard at all, registers as little more than background rustle. Even so, I was subliminally pleased to think that I'd be making a good impression on our guest.

In due course, sweet engrossment gave way to a sensation of effort. Instead of savoring sentences and paragraphs, I felt now that I was having to force the words into my mind, like herding ants into a glass vial. I'd hit a wall. Then, as now, I sub-vocalized, heard the words in my mind as I read, and the more tired I became, the more the hum and buzz of the world forced itself back into consciousness, the harder it became to hear the words, to resolve them into patterns of sense. I slogged on for a while, but only to maximize adult approval, and then put the book down on the table.

"You didn't read for very long," said the guest.

I felt deflated, humiliated, but puzzled too; if that was a short read, how long did long readers read for? I was genuinely tired from my effort and could not possibly have read for longer than that.

—∞—

Tristram Shandy, as well as being a vast and endlessly inventive cesspool of recondite smutty innuendo, is an expanded, several-layered intellectual gag, including:

1. A philosophical gag: a play on Locke's theory of the Association of Ideas according to which consciousness is comprised of endlessly and diversely associating patterns of ideas, images and experiences;

2. A literary gag: a parody of the realist novel's aspiration to describe a full "slice of life," leaving nothing out;

3. A literary-philosophical gag: a game played with the autobiographer's aspiration to lay the entire self bare in print, again leaving nothing out;

4. A psychological gag: implying that it is precisely where we might most seek to find out about ourselves that we are likely, digressively, to deflect ourselves from doing so, so that we are always chasing both our tail and our tale;

5. A cognitive gag: suggesting, as postmodern writers nowadays do, that printed language isn't a transparent medium for communication and representation but rather a *medium* that muddies what it communicates and addles the brain as the letters go in.

I think that the last three of the above are particularly pertinent to the current——what?, investigation?——insofar as I am trying to understand why print—whether I'm writing or reading it—*feels* so formidable to me—and why if reading and writing are so exhausting I chose to be a man of letters for a living—and how all of this relates to my self, "being me"——and whether I am my-self a sort of tilter at windmills (Yorick's horse, like Quixote's is named Rocinante)—driven by an obsession—what Sterne calls a "Hobby-Horse" chasing my tail and tale—never really getting anywhere——doing the tilting and carrying on about myself because in essence I am just a ° ° ° ° ° ° °   ° ° ° ° °

Slippery slope

I once saw an autobiographical documentary by the Singaporean-British violinist Vanessa Mae. Those unfamiliar with her will find that images online capture her, violin (usually) in hand, in various states of undress or in clinging chiffon bodysuits, emerging from the shallows by moonlight, or fiddling on skis as she hurtles down snowy slopes, and more.

The professed point of her narrative, "The Making of

Me," was to explore the sources of her remarkable musical ability and to see how much of it was attributable to "nature" and how much to "nurture." Was she a woman "on whose nature / nurture can never stick"? Or did she owe much of her accomplishment to her Tiger Mother, Pamela, whom, it becomes clear, the documentary is partly intended to assassinate? Pamela is presented as the archetypal driven and driving mother of a prodigy, whose love is conditional upon the child complying with a regimen that denies her a normal childhood and commits her to hours of practice each day. Mae concludes that regardless of how much she may or may not owe Pamela for her musical stardom, "There's a wrong way to love somebody, that's all."

At one stage, Ms. Mae submits herself to magnetic functional imaging. First she is conducted, conveyor-belt-like, into the scanning chamber, violin in hand, and has her brain patterns imaged as she fingers the violin neck with her customary left hand, and pretend-bows with her right (since there isn't room in the chamber to actually play). Then the experiment is repeated, but this time in reverse so that Mae is playing "wrong-handed." The right-way-round scan shows a smooth semicircular pattern of activation in well-defined smallish areas—discrete islands – a pattern associated with well-honed and/or natural skill. The wrong-handed scan has a large single activation zone spreading out like a bruise over roughly the same brain area. Apparently, the brain playing in reverse tries to co-opt more regions and networks to the process but fails adequately to coordinate them.

Not surprisingly, it turns out that scans can't really say whether high proficiency, as reflected in the first scan, is the product of natural aptitude, disciplined practice, or both. Common sense says both, but we don't need science for that, and so the "making of me" question remains as elusive to neurology as it does to philosophy and psychology.

But if you're desperate enough to have something explained, shortcomings in available modes of explanation don't seem to matter; and so I put my faith in a scan that would, *surely!*, make sense of moments like this ...

My eyes seem unable to take any more in. I can't fashion a sentence with any precision. My head feels full to bursting. Light hurts. Sound hurts. I can't remember what I've read or heard thirty seconds ago. I'm nauseous, shaky, drowsy. I feel intensely irritable, livid that I can't work on, but utterly defeated by my state. It's as if I've become allergic to everything, including the thing I cherish most: thinking. Often I have a toothache just above my left eyebrow.

With luck I make it to the bedroom without encountering any of the family, because in this state I can only feign normality and can be tetchy and dismissive. I close the door, the venetian blinds, turn off the light, and lie on my back with a pillow over my head. For the next hour or so I'll be unable to retain what's said to me, unable to respond to family needs, to carry out routine chores, to do anything. Often I'll doze off. After a while the whatever-it-is starts to ease, but I feel bruised and wobbly for the rest of the evening and wake the next day with nothing in the tank, gazing lethargically at print that gives nothing back. I go for a run or a walk in the park to spark some energy for work but the day will probably be a write-off for all but mowing the lawns and other mindless chores.

I set about trying to obtain a scan.

———

You might say that when playing left-handed, the virtuoso Mae becomes a "challenged" violinist. But what would that mean?

Arthur Koestler, a science biographer and autobiographer among many other things, wrote this in a chapter on Johannes Kepler, ironically enough the profoundly myopic father of modern optics and inventor of the modern astronomical telescope: "How is one to decide whether an inborn affliction will paralyse or galvanize?" The tale/tail I'm chasing seems in part to be an answer to this question.

———

Challenged?

If, say, full-blown dyslexia is a disability, there is presumably a sort of sliding scale to lesser versions or degrees of it: Koestler's "inborn affliction," notions like "challenged," and so on, seem to lie further along this scale at increasing removes from radical and irremediable incapacity. Along what axis the scale slides is a question. At some point the limitation crosses a threshold from being something that prevents me from being whom, ideally, I might "be," and becomes just part of who "I am." Even if "I am" includes being such a determined person that I find strategies for diluting the impact of the "inborn" limitation on my life, the strategies themselves become part of the way "I" live and so part of "me." And traces—perhaps large swathes – of the limitation will persist regardless of my effort to eliminate them.

Challenged:

1. a euphemism for *disabled*
2. deficient or lacking in some skill or capacity
3. a call or summons to engage in any contest, as of skill, strength, etc.
4. a demand to explain, justify, etc.

It would be absurd to say that I am lacking in a skill or capacity in the processing of words. But in making a profession of them I have taken on more of a challenge than a rapid reader and an effortless writer with a powerful memory might have done. Am I challenged to give an account of all of this? Well, yes. But by whom? "Me."

Lowering the bar

The sessions were run in a new, nondescript office building in Wembley, Perth, by a stylish and confident middle-aged Australian woman and her American husband. Jenny was all amenity, chattiness, and authority; Clark—mild-mannered, buttoned-down open-necked shirts, crisply creased jeans—shared her quietly unshakeable true-believer's certainty that what they had to offer really works; that it could change lives.

This was a speed-reading course, replete with shiny pamphlets, financially titrated plans and resource books from the US where the couple now did most of their teaching. Who patented this method I cannot remember, but our instructors had trained at the source and knew their onions. If perhaps a touch vulnerable to remunerative panaceas, they were by no means fools or charlatans. Both, I think, had been teachers earlier on.

Diane, who already read like the wind, took the course with me. Why, I cannot imagine. Her initial "baseline" speed assessments were cheetah-like; I clocked in like a sloth. Well, no, that is laying it on a bit. My speed was about that of a slow-to-average general reader. Fine, but not fast enough for the needs of a man of letters who could not read for long enough to compensate for sluggishness.

The course had its own vocab. You were supposed to "chunk" rather than follow a line from start to finish. I think this involved keeping toward the center of the page, not dallying reflectively in the margins. There was also the idea that you "chunked" texts into larger "bits." Various exercises were flashed up onto a projector screen, training one to register words instantaneously without having to scrutinize them, getting oracular equipment and neural networks attuned to messages of this or that magnitude, extracting the essence of meaning without dwelling on prepositions, and so on. And then there was a mechanical bar which, having been set just above your baseline speed, would travel down the page as you read, your eyes pursuing it as greyhounds hunt the cantilevered fake rabbit that circuits the track just a bit faster than they can run.

While Diane actually overtook the rabbit, my eyes

would try to get a head start on the bar by being fast out of the blocks, scurrying and chunking their way down the middle of the page, the dogged metal arm in grim, unrelenting pursuit. The moment my eyes strayed to a margin for a breather or to actually think about what I was reading, or to assess how my sprint was going, the thing would rear up like a tailgating hoon in a rear-vision mirror.

Off I'd scurry again, putting as much new space between my eyes and the bar as I could, all the while becoming less and less cognizant of what I was reading. This would go on for a couple of pages until my heart started to pound and the race became too much for me. I'd either pull out, citing the oracular equivalent of a torn hamstring, or let my eyes ski down the page, gloriously free of any hermeneutic responsibility, the arm now a sort of limbo bar for the fun that that can come with utter resignation.

The reading brain

Reading, such a routine part of so many lives, is actually a neurological miracle. It does not occur in our "natural state," though some neural capacities that evolved in that state—say, the capacity to divine animal footprints in patterns of twigs on the forest floor—probably play a part when we read.

It seems that various regions of the brain have been co-opted to perform this "unnatural" skill during the course of recent evolution. The Broca's area in the frontal lobe is pivotal to linguistic activity; the parietal lobe, further back, helps organize sensory perceptions, assists in linking sounds, meanings and emotions; the occipital lobe at the back of the brain contains the visual cortex, the part that our ancestors may have called up to divine those patterns among the twigs; this area helps with the recognition of letters. None of these can simply be thought of as neurological "locations" because all participate in a vast dynamic system, a network that contains sub-systems like the left parietotemporal system, so important for the decoding of words, and the left occipitotemporal area, which helps facilitate rapid, often instantaneous, access to words and fluency in reading. Then there must be memory input from the hippocampus and emotional involvement from the amygdala. And so on, almost—perhaps—to infinity.

But the efficiency of myriad transfers, syntheses of sensory and cognitive information, the crystallization of meaning as we read a word alone and then in combination – all of this depends on circuitry: the billions of synapses that transfer information between cells and how well they function. A super-efficient reader needs to have plenty of synapses in the right places and abundant supplies of the neurotransmitters that conduct signals across the synaptic cleft from one neuron to another. The brain of a challenged reader might perhaps have too few of the requisite synapses in the right places, too little of the requisite neurotransmitters when needed, too few areas on the network that activate during reading. And too few/too little can call up floods of adrenaline to compensate, to power the under-resourced process, after which an adrenaline "crash" can leave the person exhausted, as my work fatigue leaves me, or bouncing off walls, as kids diagnosed (rightly or wrongly) with ADHD are inclined to do.

Shall I go on? Yes, but not quite in this vein.

---◦◦◦---

Confessions of an autobiographical free-booter

Overwhelmed by the teeming Lockean superfluity of his material, Tristram appeals thus to his Muses:

> O ye POWERS! (for powers ye are, and great ones too)—which enable mortal man to tell a story worth the hearing—that kindly shew him, where he is to begin it,—and where he is to end it,—and what he is to leave out—how much of it he is to cast into shade,—and whereabouts he is to throw his light!——Ye, who preside over the vast empire of biographical free-booters … [ellipsis mine]

The "biographical free-booter," like the novelist and the autobiographer, cannot alas include everything. Selection is an essential part of narrative. Samuel Beckett's narrator-protagonist in *Molloy* puts it nicely: selection requires you to "choose, between the things not worth mentioning and those even less so." Tristram, so much a stranger to selection, is aware that his digressive inclusiveness—an approach that brings his five-hundred-page chronicle only up to his early childhood—results in a "strange state of affairs between the reader and myself." And so he solicitously provides the reader with diagrams of his own plot structures:

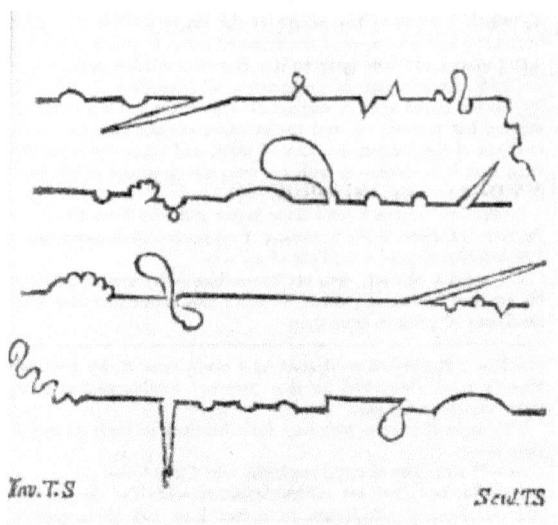

Inv. T. S   *Scul. T. S*

I, too, feel for any reader who has persisted to this point in the current inquiry and so provide you with a diagram: the homely caterpillar.

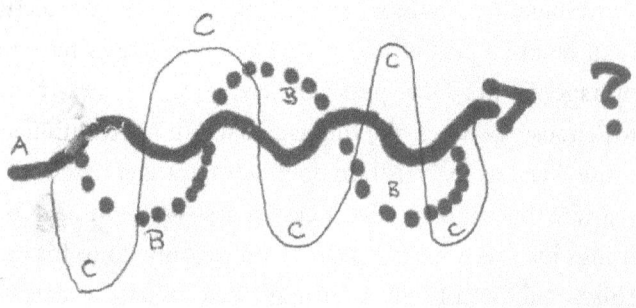

The wavy solid line "A" represents the unstable directionality of my life from birth to the point of writing, the looping dotted line "B", the way being a challenged reader who "chose" to be a man of letters augmented the directional instability of my life but also radiated out to affect the lives of those close to me, and the still more loopy thin line "C," the movement of the autobiographer's consciousness in the act of trawling through the life as expressed in "A" and "B" and trying to shape its findings into an autobiographical artifact.

Tiltings

I could put in any order an array of things I tried over thirty-five years—speed-reading, tinted glasses, meditation, self-hypnosis, exercise, pills claimed to populate and propel synaptic connections, sleep apnea surgery—to un-challenge my reading, since all—well nearly all—hit the wall—came to nothing—looped back to Square One—and indeed probably much earlier—like the "HOMUNCULUS," the him-sperm, that Tristram suspects was traumatized in the act of his conception—long before I came into being, to the gene pool whence my life emerged—a pool that contains familial dyslexia and an academic father who, though not dyslexic, was a challenged reader—just like me—but an educational neurologist finally gave me the term I was tilting for—and I write it in "tall, opake" letters: **COGNITIVE FATIGUE.**

Cognitive fatigue is sometimes referred to as "a special kind of fatigue, or tiredness."

The anterior cingulate cortex starts to slow down,

partially because it's getting less dopamine, a brain chemical that activates it. This cortex is responsible for paying attention, planning activities and detecting errors. The striatum also slows down. This part of your brain plans and prevents physical activity (prevents you from pulling the trigger when you shouldn't pull the trigger). Additionally, your brainwaves are altered. Brainwaves are the electrical activity the brain produces as a result of millions of brain cells constantly firing. All these things happen regardless of how motivated or interested you are in a subject. Some of the effects of cognitive fatigue include:

- Impaired coordination
- Difficulty focusing
- Memory problems
- Decreased ability to spot errors
- Trouble controlling impulses
- Difficulty adapting to new situations
- Trouble performing jobs that require a lot of physical stamina.

Everyone gets it to some degree and a builder might find it strange that one can feel wrecked from a day's study, but if I get whopping doses of it faster than most who do what I do, it should show up in a scan, right?

Neology or neurosis?

The reader might, I realize, wonder whether my neurological speculations aren't something of a smokescreen and whether, in fact, there might be more to all of this challenged-reader business than I'm letting on, not least to myself. Or perhaps it is *I* who am wondering this? Beckett's Molloy says, "A man like me cannot forget, in his evasions, what it is he evades." So let us try another tack.

Much has been written about the psychology—the so-called "psychodynamics"—of reading, none better perhaps than Simon Lesser's *Fiction and the Unconscious*, written over fifty years ago. Lesser's Freudian discussion is particularly concerned with literary fiction, especially because the way we engage—or fail to engage—with literary fiction will shed light on how we process fantasy more generally, including the ways in which personal fantasies guide our lives, relieve them of their tedium, provide vent for anger, and much else.

He argues that a fear of fantasy, and so of literary fiction, "reflects the misgivings of an ego which is weak, or feels itself so, about its capacity to control roused emotions." Conversely:

> when a story ensnares us and transports us to the special world it has created … The indispensable condition of such an experience, and the first stage of the experience itself, is a relaxation of the vigilance usually exercised by the ego.

Ego vigilance will, of course, show up in many other aspects of the life of a person whose ego is too vigilant.

They may be perpetually on guard, find it hard to relax, to switch off the incessant inner chatter and self-monitoring that goes on in their head. Beckett's tilters, Molloy et al., seem to need the chatter, and indeed to share it with others, as a sort of substitute Cartesian guarantee that they are alive: they are "not spared by the mad need to speak, to think, to know where one is" in their own narratives.

Since I am such a person, maybe my challenged reading is psychological rather than strictly neurological in origin? A Lesserian reading might go like this:

> Imagine an intensely aspirational but fragile boy to whom books are both fascinating and dangerous: fascinating because he loves ideas and their narrative expression; dangerous because, though highly esteemed in the world of his childhood, they become associated with his father's disappointment and depression at what he saw as his failure to fulfill his academic and career potential. The boy has an archetypal impulse to complete the task the father has left incomplete – a boy's naturally competitive instinct to outdo the father—but also a guilty fear of surpassing him lest this deepen the father's unhappiness. The father's situation is largely caused by a lack of confidence, and the boy, modeling on this, but also on the father's huge aspirational energy, is himself under-confident in taking on his task. Books—in this case works of fiction, and of intellectually powerful fine scholarship—are both attractive and intimidating. In the project

of emulation lies the possibility of failure, of not measuring up.

I'm in full stride now, like the prosecutor in *The Brothers Karamazov*, whose glorious address to the jury appears to be forensic and rhetorical perfection itself. The evidence seems to fit the theory. The theory seems to fit the evidence. ("It is the nature of a hypothesis, when once a man has conceived it, that it assimilates everything to itself, as proper nourishment," says Tristram.) And yet, Dmitri Karamazov did not kill his father, and I can listen to audio books, as I do these days, of *Tristram Shandy*, for hours on end with good recall and no fatigue. So the processing problem seems to be with those "tall opake" things—written words—rather than with subjection to the fantasies, stories and theories of others.

But there is also a possibility that does not fall within Lesser's purview: symptom as alibi. Could I, still shadowed by my father's self-doubt, have brought this symptom on all this while? Was I providing myself with an "out" if my exorbitant aspirations were not matched by my accomplishments? I really would be—

o o o o o o o o o o o o

o o o o o o o o o o o o

o o o if that was what had been going on all along.

But here I really *am* chasing my tail/tale because such psychic deviousness would cover its tracks too well for chronicling, except perhaps on an analyst's couch, and no such couch has disclosed anything this fiendish or weird. Having done so much to push through and diffuse the reading and writing issue, and having worked so hard, I really doubt that I've been secretly thwarting myself all along.

⁓

The autobiographer's hobbyhorse is forensic in its way: an attempt to run the self to ground, to redress at last the rift between narrator and protagonist, get the big questions about this life answered, loop the writing self back into a state of perfect coincidence with whom he or she writes about ("I shall never overtake myself—," bemoans Tristram.) Beckett's Moran seems to be on assignment to apprehend Molloy. But is he?

> From their places masses move, stark as laws.
> Masses of what? One does not ask. There
> somewhere man is too, vast conglomerate of all
> of nature's kingdoms, as lonely and as bound.
> And in that block the prey is lodged and thinks
> himself a being apart.

They may be parts of the same person, split off and in deadly blind pursuit of one another, if indeed in Beckett's "Trilogy" (beginning with *Molloy*, followed by *Malone Dies*, concluded by *The Unnamable*) there is personhood in the sense that we customarily think of it. The narrator in *The Unnamable*, a postmodernist work, says that he is making it all up in order to reassure himself that his life has location and direction: "I invented it all, in the hope it would console me, help me to go on, allow me to think of myself as somewhere on a road, moving, between a beginning and

122

an end." His—the novel's—last words are "I can't go on, I'll go on." Postmodernists often see Sterne, too, as one of their own, inventing it all and flaunting the fact that he's doing it. Yes and no. In *Tristram Shandy* there's a truth-like *something* at "the bottom of the well"—something about the good-heartedness of people and the naked truth of mortality: in the later stages the current, writing Tristram breaks into the narrative to reveal that he (like Sterne himself) is dying of consumption: "DEATH himself knocked at my door—ye bad him come in again; and in so gay a tone of careless indifference, did ye do it, that he doubted his commission"———, and now it dawns on us that this infinitely digressive "autobiographer" is equally compelled to tell his story and to forestall doing so: tell, because he has, however parodically, the philosophical and literary bug of total inclusion, the drive to chronicle the entire story of the self; forestall, because to catch his tail, to catch concertedly up to his adult self, would be to swing attention—ours and his—right over to his impending end. The slower the early telling the less the story threatens to end.

Migraine!!!

"Here, have a look at it," said Ken the neurologist, rotating his computer screen to face me so that I could see the scan he'd ordered of my brain. "A healthy brain, so far as the scan can see."

I didn't know enough neurology really to understand what I was looking at, but there seemed to be ample white matter and the organ appeared to be occupying an appropriate amount of my skull.

"Good. But this is a standard scan; I wonder whether magnetic functional imaging would show abnormalities when I read?"

"I doubt it," he said, "but even if it did, what's the point? It's unlikely to help with a solution. And anyway, I can't just order functional imaging for you. Only a few places do it and only a few people can access it for patients."

He wasn't being unsympathetic. Indeed, he found my case interesting and we had something of a history; curiously enough, his father had been my father's Head of Department during the time of his Honors degree in Politics at the University of Melbourne and when he started teaching there. It was after this point that he veered off into careers that didn't suit him—things like advertising, stockbroking, a managerial position in a state power instrumentality.

"Do you get migraines?" Ken inquired.

"No," I said, "but I do get bad sinus headaches which are like a toothache above my left eyebrow and sometimes spread right across my forehead."

"Well, hold on," he said. "Does a Professor of English know the difference between a sinus headache and a migraine?"

After I'd recounted my long history of sinus trouble and surgery, he reckoned that, even so, the fatigue symptoms I got from reading could well be caused by migraines. It might go something like this: deficient circuitry could stress the brain in ways that caused "vascular agitation" and thus migraine. The causes of the deficit were probably undiscoverable, though they could be partly genetic.

This sounded very plausible and I left, cheered, with a script for migraine medication in hand, though not a referral for the holy grail of magnetic functional imaging.

Meanwhile I read Oliver Sacks' superb treatise on the subject, *Migraine*. It was hugely informative but also fatiguing: its 320 pages of small print gave me a headache – indeed, if Ken was right, a migraine.

Migraine lifts the etiology of migraine into a new quasi-Darwinian dimension. The book, a marvelous synthesis of modern neurology, Freud, Darwin and much else, sees migraine as both a biological and a cultural phenomenon, and as arising from highly complex interactions between these two causal domains. Speaking of primitive biological survival responses, Sacks writes:

> This then is the hinterland of biological reactions from which we conceive migraines to have arisen in the course of evolution, and to have become with the elaboration of human nervous systems and human needs, progressively differentiated and refined.

And again:

> We envisage that psychosomatic reactions, like neurotic defenses, have become not only more necessary with the increasing complexity and repressiveness of civilized life, but also more versatile and sophisticated: thus, the simple

protective reflexes we have discussed may evolve into the richly allusive, over-determined and protean migraines so common in present society.

We tend to think of illness as malfunction rather than as survival adaptation. But surely it was good for the twig-diviner and his tribe that he got crippling headaches if he stayed out too long, peered fiercely at those patterns in failing light, and had to chill out in the cave for a few days to recoup. Better for him; better for the tribe who needed his powers of divination.

⸺⸳⸺

Let us at last get round to the magnetic functional imaging scan!

Here are three possibilities:

1.   At the time of writing I have still not managed to access such a scan.

2.   After my stint in Vanessa Mae's vault, the neurologist says:

Well, some areas we'd expect to light up a lot in a man with your skills are a bit dim and the pattern of activation is a bit diffuse, but we simply aren't in a position to say at this point whether these results are just within or a bit beyond the normal range, and, either way, what it means. Certainly the scan doesn't show anything wildly unusual, anything to be worried about.

3.   After my stint in Mae's vault, the neurologist says:

Well, I don't wonder you get those symptoms.

The scan is actually quite abnormal. Big pools of activation light up when you read and write—much bigger than in a normal reader. This does suggest an underlying inefficiency in the circuitry, which the brain has to spend an enormous amount of energy compensating for by co-opting back-up regions. The brain already uses more energy than any other organ in the body, so this extra load would indeed exhaust you, would explain your acute cognitive fatigue. I'm not sure whether there is a migrainous process involved, and you've tried all the treatments we have at this point. But, for what it's worth, you have the peace of mind that comes with confirmation—and my sympathies.

—⁂—

One of Sacks' case histories even refers to a middle-aged academic:

> *Case 75*: A middle-aged professor, of fiery temperament, who tends to get classical migraines on Friday afternoons, following his inspired and stormy teaching sessions. He has scarcely time to rush home from these before scotomata [dramatic disturbance in visual field] and other symptoms make their appearance, followed within minutes by violent hemicrania [headache on one side of the head], nausea, and vomiting. If these symptoms are *endured*, they run their course and resolve in three hours, leaving a wonderful sense

of refreshment, and almost of rebirth. If, on the other hand, they are *aborted* (as they may be by ergotamine, exercise, or sleep), there is a persistent malaise throughout the entire weekend. Thus this patient is presented with a *choice*: to be violently ill for three hours, and then perfectly well; or to be vaguely ill and wretched for two to three *days*. Since realizing his situation, he has given up the use of all abortive measures, finding a severe but brief migraine altogether preferable to a mild but greatly extended one.

This, of course, isn't my case, but clearly this academic's capacity to give "inspiring" lectures was deeply implicated in his susceptibility to migraines: his passionate intensity helps to account for both, and the latter gave him protection—forced him to chill out in the cave—when his temperament might have caused him, say, to have a stroke and disable his inspirational teaching.

This man, indeed, decided not to take the medication that would moderate but also extend his migraine. He preferred to embrace the self that could feel sick as a dog for a shortish while and then gloriously alive when the malady lifted. This was adaptation in a sense that goes well beyond mere survival: it's about knowing how to live, how to *flourish*.

―∞∞∞―

This chapter—mine, I mean—is giving me a headache. Let me, reader, try to get hold of it, by tail, tale or perhaps, better still, head …

There is no doubt that reading and writing is easier for me than some—and harder than for some—and that I've given myself and those around me—literally it would seem—a headache by choosing a profession that was bound to make me feel often crummy and irritable—but—what a pain I'd have been if I'd done something I didn't have a passion for. I loved it even as it knocked me around: passion's etymology—to suffer, to endure, but also to desire.—But where is the head, tail, tale in this?—Doing it in the only way I knew how helped *make me*—but I read that way because of who I (already?) was?—and being/having become such a person I was bound (as in bondage?) to write to find meaning in "life"—and here I am/I am writing—about it all. Yes, it gives me a headache but to say I was "challenged" is a bit rich, isn't it?!—given the talents I was given. The life I've had—

This whole "mistook" business is a mistake. Maybe, as Koestler says, I was "galvanized" by having to read slow—got intimate with text in a way a speed-reader wouldn't—and maybe being so intimately acquainted with resistance, difficulty, fatigue, made me the sort of reader and writer I am——for better and for worse—and to dream of being the sort of speed-reader with a photographic memory who steps—fresh as a daisy—out of his study each evening—maybe this is just to dream of being someone else——and if there was a mistake it was turning life into an exam instead of just doing something worthwhile because it *was*—the Fates forbid!——*worthwhile.*

When next we encounter a wall in *Tristram Shandy*, toward halfway in the narrative, it is again two-sided, but this time, in the original editions, it is in the form of marbled paper that has long been used at the beginning and end of well-produced books: in this case, red, yellow, various tones of brown, pinkish tan, black, white, and more. It is, Tristram says, the "most motley emblem of my work"—a comment as much beyond dispute as it is elucidation.

———

Of course, ten years hence—if I live that long—there may be more sophisticated scans—better synthetic neurotransmitters—more industrial-strength migraine medications—vastly improved understanding of the neurology cognition——and——

Shall I go on?—NO————

PS The scan outcome was: 1. Not having a serious illness, I could not access one.

Seven

Sauna talk

I long
To hear the story of your life, which must
Take the ear strangely.

—Shakespeare, *The Tempest*

All animals are equal, but some animals are more
equal than others.

—George Orwell, *Animal Farm*

In my teens and twenties I'd get so depressed I could barely drag myself out of bed. I'd been pretty much free of such troughs for three decades; but now, as I approached sixty, I was starting to feel the old putrid gloom again. The family had gone home and I was seeing out my contract at a university in Hong Kong for the remaining year. I'd never been any good at solitude, which for me always seemed to sour into loneliness; the department I was running was a mess; and I'd moved out of the lovely three-bedroom apartment the family had been renting right on the South

China Sea. I was already missing the lapping of the water in the marina beneath our balcony, and close proximity to the chrome, glass, and marble Leisure Center a few hundred meters of manicured lawn away, with its sauna and its resort-style pool nestling among the palms.

The apartment to which I returned, lonely and anxious after work each day, was on the sixteenth floor of a peeling old high-rise and was tiny. Between two adjoining residential towers you could catch a framed view of the sea from the living room window, though the smog that engulfed Hong Kong for most of the year reduced this to a filmy Turneresque haze, smudging out the horizon, leaving junks and giant cargo ships suspended in inky air. The best view had been reserved for a window opposite the lift in a grimy tiled thoroughfare where you'd only pause to find your keys.

The double bed occupied almost my entire bedroom and at its foot a battered TV sat on a chest of drawers. Prone to electrical storms, it was as indispensable as it was unreliable; when alone I was no better at "death's counterfeit," as Macduff so aptly calls sleep, than I was at being awake.

I'd switch on the old air conditioner above the bed, its rattling gusts of stale air oddly soothing until the racket started ringing in my ears. Then I'd reach for the TV remote. If my luck was in there'd be a test match on the Indian cricket channel, or an episode of "Jurassic Fight Club" on the Discovery Channel where lovingly fashioned animations of prehistoric monsters tore each other limb from limb or gulped smaller life forms down like *hors d'oeuvres*.

The 2008 US presidential election campaign was underway. The more moderate news networks could see some of Obama's remarkable qualities and what it would mean to put an African-American in the White House; but now, roaming cable in the bad hours, I discovered Fox News, the main media outlet for the American Far Right. Who *were* these people? And why did I persist in watching such lunacy when I was in poor shape?

A particular torment was *Fox & Friends*, a fireside three-some on an L-shaped sofa. There was Gretchen Carlson, an American-Scandinavian former Miss World, blonde hair an armored gloss; Brian Kilmeade, pouting lower lip, tight-curled feathery hair; and, most egregious of all, Mr. Steve Doocey, stork-necked, tall, blond and angular, a WASP pterodactyl of the airwaves, all seething charm and viperous hatred of anything that might ruffle his vast sense of patrician entitlement.

They'd harp on about Obama's former pastor, sneeringly inquire "what *is* community organizing anyway?", question Obama's patriotism, deride his intellectual accomplishments. The "friends" who joined them on the sofa were a hellish lot: white lawyers and Republican operatives railing about fraud in Obama's campaign; bizarrely coiffured "columnists" branding him a Muslim, and a would-be terrorist; former Bush aides, undaunted by eight disastrous years in power, dispensing political advice; Far Right website columnists; clearly deranged "constitutionalists" convinced that Obama would take their guns and hand the US over to jihadists. And, perhaps most bizarre of all, smooth black rhetoricians who charged Obama with every sin under the sun and seemed to want nothing more than to keep the White House white.

I'd doze, periodically waking, miserable and disoriented in the early hours with Fox still on. Now the anchor would be Sean Hannity, cable's triceratops, with his armored bull neck, bullet head, and hair that thrust up to one side like a fan. Once he roused me from sleep ranting at a guest: "America is the greatest country in the world! America is the greatest country in the world!"

It had been a particularly bad day in the Department. A colleague had gone berserk at me, literally frothing at the mouth. I felt I was leaning too heavily on friends at the University for support, and that stress and depression were causing me to make administrative mistakes. I left campus as soon as I could, caught a ramshackle old minibus back to the apartment, changed, and set off in the clinging late-afternoon heat for the Leisure Center, a fifteen-minute walk away.

Swinging its heavy glass doors open, I was greeted by a gust of cold air and beheld people of all ages milling about in the foyer: air hostesses awaiting the airport bus, ping-pong paddle-swishing kids fresh from lessons, mums collecting toddlers from child care, retirees in armchairs browsing the papers, lithe young bodies glistening from the gym. Through the glass wall at the back of the foyer the palm-lined resort pool sparkled in the fierce sun. Here, with goggles on, I'd float facedown, arms outstretched, gazing at the aqua tiles that lined the pool's underbelly, drifting, like Proust's memory-sedimented swimmer, between various installments of myself—a carefree kid like those splashing around me, the anxious middle-aged man that I was now, the future self, like those lounging on chairs in the shade beside the pool. Proust says with glorious and typical extravagance of his swimmer:

> For man is that ageless creature who has the faculty of becoming many years younger in a few seconds, and who, surrounded by the walls of time through which he has lived, floats within them as in a pool the surface-level of which is constantly changing so as to bring him within range now of one epoch, now of another.

After a long "swim" I'd ease back in the sauna, which was tucked away in a quiet part of the men's change rooms. Just now I badly needed to be alone, to regather some balance, and the sauna was usually empty at this hour.

I'd just settled on the wooden bench beside a potted fern and a cauldron of sizzling stones, the baking heat and scent of pine starting to defuse a knot of tension in my chest, when another gust of refrigerated air signaled company.

There stood a bald man of perhaps seventy-five, completely naked save for a gaggle of chains and pendants about his neck, his ample belly shading his sparsely whiskered manhood. Perhaps he'd just come from the gym, because sweat was streaming down his long arms, chest, back and thighs.

I could have done without this, but his "Hi there!" was friendly enough, and Americans were usually interesting to talk to.

"Nice to see you," said I, wishing that I hadn't seen quite so much.

A sign on the sauna door requested users to sit on a towel or to be covered. So my Speedos nestled under my own ample belly, like a black nylon ribbon bedecking an Easter egg. But my companion, seeing no need for such niceties, parked his buttocks directly onto the pine paling a few feet to my left.

What, I wondered, had this stranger to hygiene done for a living? "I'd guess you're retired," I ventured. "What was your line of crime?"

"Well," he said, "I was a doctor."

I must have looked surprised because he quickly elaborated: he was a GP who had practiced for fifty years in a small town outside Austin, Texas. He still saw patients from time to time, and he was in Hong Kong visiting his son.

My curiosity was aroused and with the US elections so much on my mind I wondered how a man like this might vote. "So, who do you like—McCain or Obama?"

"Well, I'll tell ya," he said. "I don't want too much change. I'm for McCain. I hope he can get us out of Iraq, do OK with the economy, be a steady guy. I think he can. I'll be voting for him."

"You have reservations about Obama?"

"Obama's a bright guy and a great orator, but I'd never vote for a black man. Nothing against black people, but I've had a lot of black patients and they're too emotional. They got a chip on their shoulder that makes them emotional. Always thinking people are racists trying to take them down. You ask my black patients and they'll tell you that I'm no racist. I care for them just like I care for my white patients. I like black people and they can't help their history. But their history makes them too emotional to be president. That's why I'll never vote for a black man."

The Texan in *Catch 22* came to mind—a man brimming with friendly talk and retrograde political ideas, whose monologues emptied military hospital wards.

But I took his declaration in as calmly as I could and was about to argue the point when something about his face made me desist. It was round but jowly, weatherworn and blotched with sunspots. His gray-blue eyes, as he delivered his views, were self-assured, steady, but by no means steely. I didn't think I saw hatred. He seemed more artless and frank than a Doocey. But …

"Do you really mean *never*? Never's a long time. Maybe an Obama presidency would change the race thing in your country? Put blacks more at their ease?"

"Never!" he shot back. "I'll be long gone before black people get all that suspicion out of their systems. When they do, some other folks can vote for them. Maybe my grandchildren. But not me. *Never!*"

What could one say? I felt the mild condescension of

an academic listening to a simple man—albeit, alas, an educated one—delivering himself of ignorant thoughts. The laptop moralist in me wanted to talk his views down, but again something—maybe a kind of pity, or a disinclination to judge one from a world I scarcely knew—caused me to hold back.

I tried to imagine him five decades earlier, picturing his bald head well-thatched with a young man's hair and his dilapidated body taut with energy. I had a flickering image of broad shoulders, a straight back, a muscled frame. Then, as the man before me edged again into focus, I noticed that one of the icons draped about his neck was a crucifix. Here was my chance.

"You know St Augustine?"

"Sure I know him. I'm a Catholic. He's one of the greatest men in the Church."

"Well, of course, you'll know he was a colored man—an African?"

"No kidding!" he said. "Augustine a black man! Sir, I never knew that! I've never seen a painting of him."

"There are images, but the ones I've seen don't seem to dwell on his skin color. As you can imagine."

"Well, I'll be!" he said. "I got a cousin in an Augustinian order. I'll ask him about it."

I didn't like the me that was manipulating the conversation now, examining him, lauding my learning over a man of such limited understanding. But still I wasn't done. I was about to point out that Augustine was one of the greatest—and, yes, most *rational*—thinkers in Western history, when my eyes, which had been surveying his various chains and trinkets, spotted a jagged scar that ran from his right breast bone down his chest almost to the base of his rib cage. Seeing that I was staring at his disfigurement, he said, "I nearly died." And, drawing the chains aside like a little metallic curtain, "There are more where that came from."

Indeed there were: his chest was crisscrossed with scars, their raised edges reminiscent of a whipping.

"Do you mind my asking what happened?"

"I don't mind, sir."

He leaned back, drawing his hands along his thighs and looking straight ahead into the steam. "There I was—a healthy man of sixty, on my daily walk, feeling fit as I'd been at thirty, when *wham!* I get this huge pain in my chest and arm. My wife says I toppled onto the road and almost got run down, but next thing I wake up in hospital with her holding my hand saying that I've had a heart attack and the doctor will be in to talk to me soon. She's looking real upset so I start wondering how bad the attack was."

He half-turned toward me, perspiration beading on the tip of his nose, his mouth slightly twisted as if in distaste.

"The doctor, I knew the guy. I knew him well. A cardiologist I used to send my own patients to. I had confidence in this guy. When he came in I said straight away, 'Was it a bad one?' and he tells me, 'It was a bad one.' He says, 'One artery completely blocked, another almost as bad. I've done an angioplasty and put in two stents, but you almost died and there's a lot of damage to the heart muscle. You're gonna need a transplant.'

"I almost had another attack there and then. Maybe he could have cushioned the blow a bit, but I was in his hands and that's how he gave out the news."

I tossed some water on the steaming rocks and sat down again. His eyes sought mine and, satisfied that he still had my attention, he looked away again.

"I was taken to Point View hospital for observation. I was waiting for days for the doctors to decide whether I needed a transplant. One day it was 'yes,' next day it was 'no, but more surgery.' They were tough days, wondering what they were gonna do and how much time I might have left. But then the doctors decided I didn't need a transplant. I had two more operations and here I am, fit, and making sure I stay that way."

I wondered how fit he could be at his present weight and whether the rigors of a sauna were really good for him. But who was I to wonder? He was the doctor, though, oddly, when he'd described his time as a patient his professional identity had vanished. He'd become just another sick guy waiting for "the doctors" to decide his fate, his body as alien as the octopus to which Proust likens the ill body.

He sat motionless as if pondering his own story for a while, rose unsteadily to his feet, said, "Well, nice talking to you," and let himself out through the glass door.

I sat back on the bench trying to make sense of him.

A few minutes later I stepped out of the sauna into the

change room on the way to the pool. There he was to my left, lolling abstractedly on a bench, still stark naked, still streaming with sweat, cooling himself in the chilled air. We exchanged friendly nods. *Should I ask him about Fox News?* Somehow I didn't have the heart. He looked tired, even frail now.

Something had passed between us. He'd been frank with me; he'd quite trustingly shared important pieces of his life story. But what sort of trust was this? The confidence one white man reposes in another in a foreign place, surrounded by people of another race? Still, just when I'd thought I least wanted company we'd been fleeting companions of a sort; indeed, that human connection had even momentarily taken the edge off my distress. Yet how could you like a man who held such views …?

But, still feeling a kind of pity, I gave him a thumbs-up and smiled wanly as I shuffled past him. He smiled tiredly back.

The pool was lovely and cool and I paddled about aimlessly for some time, almost oblivious to splashing kids and the determined adults swimming laps. But I felt flat, empty and anxious; and the feeling clung as I trudged back to the apartment and ate a solitary meal, flicking through texts and emails.

The thought of bed was almost intolerable. Perhaps I'd roam the compound and strike up a conversation at a bar? No, the last thing I wanted now was company. One thing was for sure—I wouldn't be watching Fox tonight. I hoped I wouldn't spiral down during the night and wake too miserable and enervated to face the day.

I thought again with an odd mixture of aversion, incredulity, and care about the old doctor from Texas.

And I hoped like hell that Obama would be president.

Eight

The black dog

Leo's life

> Psychoanalysts are missing important clues about patients' childhoods if they do not ask about the dogs the patients knew.

> —Kurt Vonnegut, *Palm Sunday*

> Argos passed into the darkness of death, now that he had seen his master once more after twenty years.

> —Homer, *Odyssey*

He came well recommended: "Yes, he's a nice little dog," said the vet who had performed his de-sexing operation when the black short-haired bitzer was handed in at the pound.

I'd rung because much as I wanted a new dog, I had to be careful: Madeleine, who adored dogs, was only three at the time and would need an even-tempered pet; the new acquisition would have to spend long stretches alone in the backyard while we were at work; and my father, who was fond of dogs, had rapid-onset dementia and was now easily alarmed by unexpected or boisterous activity.

Our previous pooch, a remarkable collie-border-collie-cross named Issy (after a distant cousin of mine who was a celebrated violinist), had died shortly before we left Perth the previous year.

Issy was a black long-haired sage among canines with a white beard-like fringe about his muzzle. He'd been devoted to Maddie since her arrival, summoning us to her bedroom if we hadn't heard her crying, keeping the inquisitive cat at a safe distance from the cot. He'd also been a sweet source of emotional security for Ben, as the young boy shuttled between the houses of his re-married parents.

Issy's greatest love, until a torn knee ligament restricted him later in life to trotting beside me on walks and jogs, was chasing a tennis ball. I'd scoop the ball up with a twisted old wooden racquet, flick it off the strings into the air high enough to launch a forehand at it, and watch this supreme athlete hurtle after it. Chewing it with his long pointy jaws he'd deposit the ball at my feet, look triumphantly up at me, then back away, poised for another dash. In truth, the pleasure in this simple pastime was mutual: I enjoyed flipping the ball from one side of the racquet to the other without changing my grip on the handle, then imparting topspin or backspin on the shot, or smashing it for maximum distance and release of pent-up energies. Top spin would arc high, drop sharply and jump on landing, the pooch leaping three and four feet to snatch it at the top of its bounce. Backspin's shallower arc, drifting tempo and lower bounce, often enabled the pursuer to snaffle it in his jaws without breaking stride. The flat low hard hits, which made the ball run-on fast when it touched down, required a late killer sprint from Issy. His aerobic capacities seemed almost limitless.

But finessing the ball with that twisted old racquet was just part of the fun. Issy's sheer delight was pleasure of the purest ilk—beautiful to see and beautiful for me, because he *was* me, off adulthood's leash, flying through parks after any ball that could be hit, kicked or hurled. The American poet and memoirist of canines, Mark Doty, says of his two dogs that they were "the secret heroes of my vitality." Issy was, in some measure, the secret hero of mine.

So smart was that beautiful creature that when I played tennis with a human combatant he would lie against the back fence of the court, somehow understanding that a racquet-propelled ball was not for chasing in this setting.

Issy's huge vocabulary and intuitive sensitivities enabled him to negotiate many situations, including those he shared with his human pack, but one challenge was too much even for him. Sometimes, when a slaggy tennis ball had been worn bare by crashings and chewings, it would make an odd hollow *thwack* against the racquet face and divide in mid-air, falling to ground in two separate places. The question of which half now constituted the ball was too much for him. He'd dart from one half to the other and back, until settling, for opaque reasons, on one hemisphere and depositing it at my feet.

Once, when he'd reached late middle age and his ball-chasing days were behind him, we were walking in a nearby park around a wide brown lake. As was my habit, I looked back to check that he was within whistling range and was surprised to see him lying on his side fifty meters away. It was a hot Perth late afternoon, but this, I thought, was a touch excessive even in an aging dog with long thick fur. I was a bit impatient as I approached. But when I got to him and tried to ease him to his paws I realized that something was wrong. I eventually lifted him into the back of the car and took him to the local vet—an avuncular former footballer—who was unsure what to make of his condition and suggested that I leave him there overnight for observation. I felt bad about this, but after waiting for quite a while I allowed myself to be persuaded that if a serious "event" were to occur during the night he would be safer in the animal hospital than at home.

First thing next morning I drove back. The vet said he was "very sorry." During the night, Issy had suffered a major heart attack, was now in a coma, and could not be saved. I went to his cage and looked in. Issy's eyes were milky and vacant. No sign of recognition. I sat down on one of the white plastic chairs in the waiting room, stunned. The vet said that the dog would probably not be feeling any pain at this stage, that the end was very near, but that it would be kindest to bring it on with an injection. I stood and watched as the green toxin fed through a clear tube extinguished Issy's life.

I have never forgiven myself for leaving that creature,

so deeply and trustingly bonded to me, to spend his final hours dying in that cage, alone. Whenever I think of it, it goes through me like a spear.

---⊗⊗⊗---

Animal-loving philosopher and memoirist Raimond Gaita argues that "The attenuated nature ... of individuality in animals shows most clearly perhaps in the fact that we do not write biographies of animals." He says that we do "tell stories about animals, as I do in this book, but the stories do not add up to a biography because nothing counts as Orloff [his first dog] or Gypsy [his current one] or Jack the cockatoo making or failing to make something of their lives, nor even of life making something of them ... They cannot rejoice in their life nor can they despair of it."

In other words, biography, or at least biography as it is spoken of in common parlance, requires a particular kind of interior life in the biographical subject—a kind that is in principle ascertainable or about which we can at least make informed speculations, and one that involves at least two features that we associate with the inner lives of human beings: the ability to conceptualize a life (as, say, wasted or triumphant) and to make deliberation-based decisions within the framework of that conceptualization. For Gaita, biographies, as distinct from "stories," can only be framed about individual entities that meet these requirements.

Do dogs have the capacity to conceptualize their lives? I don't know, but it wouldn't surprise me if a dog on the last rung of the pack, surviving on desiccated scraps after the rest have finished eating, spending much of its life alone without physical contact with other pack members, might think something to the effect of *this is a lousy life*, or that a stray taken in by a loving family might reflect in doggy terms that *this beats the hell out of how it was before and this is the life I want.*

Gaita seems to have ruled out such possibilities, *a priori*: "I do not believe that the animals I have written about had reflective capacities." And, again, this time of Gypsy: "I'm quite sure she doesn't think anything." In the spirit of rich and intricate discussion we could go on refining our terms—probing, for instance, the relationship between the notions of "reflection" and "thought," and between each of these and human language and concepts—but the fact is that we don't finally know and that many dog owners, myself included, have an intuitive sense that these uncanny animals *do* have a concept of the life they are living and that, given their enormous receptiveness to human modes of existence, their concepts can be influenced in some ways by ours, as ours, I believe, are by theirs.

I'd argue that Gaita's concept of biography is too limited even for some human lives. Take for instance the parent of a profoundly intellectually disabled child—one with no discernible conceptualized or conceptualizing inner life—who decides to write that child's "biography." Here the very choice of a term with the cultural cachet of "biography" may be salient, since one of the parent's aims in writing is to confer significance and dignity on the life of one who cannot speak for herself and will tend to be seen according to current social attitudes as living a diminished or lesser life. The parent would have the child leave a footprint in the sand. Even if the parent were convinced that the child had no conceptual life whatsoever, there would still be a history of perceived and communicated feelings—distress and pleasure, among others—worthy of biographical report. Biography could also record how that child *mattered*, if not to herself as someone self-consciously living a conceptualized life, then certainly to *others*—parents, siblings, other relatives, carers, and so on—who formed deep (and perhaps reciprocated) attachments with her. Pets, I believe, "matter" in these ways as well.

———

Biographical inquiry into the new dog's early life yields only scattered details, some of them perhaps apocryphal. It is not known when or where he was born, nor what circumstances greeted his arrival. He seems first to have entered recorded human consciousness when discovered wandering thin, lost, and without identification, in an alpine reserve several hours from Melbourne. One supposition—that he was dumped there by people who had no use for him—seems plausible, but cannot be confirmed. From there he was apparently conducted to a pound in Melbourne and sentenced to death by a certain date if not claimed or adopted. At this point he acquired a guardian angel by the name of Pam, who removed him to a dog shelter she ran in the suburbs. It was in response to word of mouth about Pam that we knocked on her door in the winter of 1991.

As it happened, Pam lived in a beautifully maintained

brick Edwardian home just a couple of streets from the park in which I played football and cricket as a boy. As this immaculately coiffured surgeon's wife opened the door, a pack of dogs of various breeds, shapes, and sizes issued a cacophonous welcome (or perhaps warning), those who had made it first to the tasteful wood-framed wire veranda door, scrabbling claws against its now bulging mesh. Even I, so deeply at ease around dogs, found this a touch confronting. Ben, not wanting to be seen shirking an issue, stayed close beside me; dog-loving Maddie hid behind dog-wary Diane, who was doing her best to disappear behind me, one hand clutching the back of my sweater.

Pam, dogs pawing at her tweed skirt and woolen cardigan, conducted us down an airy carpeted corridor and into a genteel sitting room, where she offered us tea and biscuits. I sat Maddie high on my lap to keep her shortbread cookies and Tim Tams well out of canine reach. Ben held his biscuits safely aloft when not chomping on them. Diane wisely abstained. Pam perched on the sofa shooing the marauding pack away until she'd eaten. Then each supplicant got its reward. One dog was a short-haired, medium-sized black character of indeterminate breed, with a white stripe down his longish blunt snout, a ragged band of white fur around his neck which extended to his chest and to one front paw, and anxiously alert brown eyes. Another, also black, seemed to be a labrador augmented by genes from some gargantuan breed. Pam provided biographical details of these two in particular since they seemed most likely to meet our needs. Having heard about the smaller dog's alpine wanderings and a more reassuring account of the larger one's earlier life, we agreed that we would take the latter—named Magic—to the park for a trial outing.

And so, just where I had spent endless hours pretending to be Ron Barassi and preparing for a grand career as a footballer, we let Magic off his leash. He zoomed about in a world of his own, sometimes acknowledging our presence with bounding leaps, one of which terrified Diane. Another knocked little Maddie clean over. Sweet in his way, Magic was alas too generically "doggy" for our needs. Not without a twinge of guilt we returned him to Pam and took the smaller, as yet unnamed, white-frilled waif to the same park. He, too, flew exuberantly but in a way much more attuned to his human chaperones. Sensing Maddie's physical vulnerability, he would decelerate well before he reached her, then gently nuzzle her hands and arms, or trot along with Ben, who was about to attempt a tree that I used to climb as a boy. This little dog had bonded with the kids in what seemed like seconds. The thought of him back in a yowling cage at the pound, and then being led away to execution, was horrendous. We agreed with Pam that we'd take him home for a week and see how things went.

Our white clapboard Edwardian house, many suburbs from Pam's, was in much poorer repair than hers. Soon after we moved in we pulled up the patterned linoleum in the hallway and had the long-concealed, lovely pine floorboards beneath polished to a honeyed sheen. On this surface, the new arrival made that accelerating scrape-scuttling sound familiar to dog owners. The kids would stand at either end of the central corridor, the pooch zooming between them, pausing only for a quick pat at one end before doubling back.

It was in this hallway that he welcomed me home on my first workday after his arrival. Bounding toward me he threw himself on his back, his momentum carrying him forward for several feet, paws up, along the glossy boards. I bent over him and began to stroke that white breast which resembled a neatly positioned napkin just under his chin. I could have done with a napkin myself, because the column of urine that now arced upward like a line of spray on a revolving garden sprinkler left large blotches on my tie and sprinkled my ears and glasses on its way down to my right shoe. However unwelcome, there was something quite apposite about this greeting: it was becoming apparent that certain senior colleagues were intent on welcoming me, their young professor, in a similar way, albeit metaphorically ("More numerous than the hairs of my head are those who hate me"), though their disposition was rather less abject and respectful of my place in the pack than was Leo's. Henceforth, the canine welcoming ritual was performed in the back garden after I'd removed my coat and tie and armed myself with a large plastic sheet.

The pup quickly acquired the accouterments of canine domesticity—food and water bowls in the laundry outside the back door, the run of the large fenced-in back garden, and an assortment of beds, sofas and mats to sleep on. It was at this point too that he acquired a name—Leo. Maddie, who proposed the name, has no recollection of how or why she chose it and in truth there was nothing noticeably Leo-like about that whelp: nothing leonine, for instance, nor uproariously clubbable, a trait common in the human Leos I have known. Even when long-settled with the family, his presence was sweet, sensitive, affectionate, fun-loving, gregarious but generally submissive, as if any alpha male impulses had been quelled by his distressing start in life. But the little dog responded almost immediately to the call of his name, as if it had been threaded in his DNA.

I thought that the yard, with its high fences and high gate, would be impregnable, even to an athletic young dog, but he managed to scale the gate and dash off into unfamiliar streets soon after coming home. We dashed after him in our rattly old red Volvo, shouting his name, knocking on doors, hardly daring to look down each new street for fear of what we might see. The search must have gone on for an hour. Fearful and disconsolate we drove back to the house—and there he was, lolling peacefully on the front lawn, waiting for us as if he'd resided there for years. This was a remarkably cluey little creature, and loveable too; but I was beginning to doubt that my stress levels at the time were up to his juvenile, winning, widdling ways.

My parents were pleased to hear of the new arrival and came to visit the next weekend. Fleur, an ebullient dog lover, returned Leo's thankfully piddle-free front garden welcome with the greatest enthusiasm. But I had to keep him at bay while we helped Paul, now a stooped, white-haired old man with deceptively rosy cheeks and thick glasses, through the front door, down the long corridor, down steps into the sunken living room at the back of the house, and into a chair. Seeing him seated, Leo burst from his moorings, danced about the chair and then rose on his hind legs, attempting to lick my ill father's face. The suddenness of all of this was alarming to Paul, who was still getting his bearings in the house, and an abashed Leo was summarily grabbed, finger-wagged and put outside the back door.

Dog lovers and others will know the intense concentration that the outcast now focused on that back door as he ran through a repertoire of long and short barks, whimpers, squeaks, groans, scrabbles, and scratches. No thought of slinking off and lying in defeated isolation in the laundry. Leo eyeballed the door as a trapped miner might eyeball boulders piled between him and the safety of fresh air, family and friends.

I felt a strange pull between the bewildered, stranded young hound and my tragically ill parent—Paul, in addition to the ghastly dementia, was slowly dying of prostate cancer. But of course my father's needs came first. The pathetic canine commentary at the back door continued. And after a while, the kids and I, and their grandmother too, were overcome by it and decided to give the dog another go. I let Leo in again, having fastened him to a lead Pam had lent us. Despite being unhappy at not being completely free to schmooze with whomever he pleased, Leo was hugely relieved to be back with the pack and happily cavorted with the kids at the end of his lead. Then one of them unwittingly let the brown leather cord slip and the little dog flew about the room again, delighting the kids but again alarming my father. Feeling overcome by the enormity of Paul's condition on top of the family move and my new job, I decided, then and there, much to the kids' dismay, that Leo was too young, frisky, and insecure for us in our present situation and that he would have to go back to Pam.

And so, a couple of days later, I ushered the gay little guy, so happy and unsuspecting, into the red Volvo and returned him to her. Not surprisingly, perhaps, I have no recollection of actually leaving him there, with that pack of scrabbling, needy canines, all craving sustenance, love, security and the freedom to give vent to their limitless capacity for fun.

The last thing I needed was for Maddie to continually ask: "Why can't we have Leo back? Why did we have to give him away again? Why can't he stay outside when Poppa Paul comes to visit?"

I felt awful about giving him back—so much so that I started to question my emotional priorities: how could I be so concerned about a stray mutt when my father was in this harrowing condition? Then it occurred to me that the abandoned condition of the dog and my fine and decent father's lonely descent into a ghoulish fate were somehow entangled in my mind, that my anguish wasn't making tidy distinctions between father, son and homeless dog. Anguish, after all, has a way of making its own arrangements. Ben, too, was upset about Leo, and it was the kids who got me to think more clear-headedly about the situation.

Various tests had made it brutally clear that nothing aside from palliative care and emotional support could now be offered to Paul. He was old, desperately unlucky to have these two fearful illnesses together, and was going to die in his mid-seventies. But that little dog could be offered a good life, and the kids were right that he could be managed when their grandfather came to visit. Besides, that sweet little guy—still quite freshly minted and dying to throw himself into a life he was so superlatively fashioned to enjoy—would cheer us all up.

And so back to Pam we went. This time when she opened the door, Leo, as if knowing or hoping that it would be us, had slithered his way past bigger dogs and greeted us with a delirious desperation that lit up that gloomy day. Nor was he about to pause for farewells, not even to Pam. Leash on and the door at last open, he dragged me to the car.

The little guy didn't so much adapt to his pack as take what seemed to be his preordained place among humankind. Here was evidence for the "co-evolution" of the two species, the development of each, as the theory goes, influencing the other.

How this development occurred is much debated. Did the first non-combative interactions occur between Neanderthals and wolves, Neanderthals and wolves that had begun evolving into modern dogs, between Homo sapiens and wolves, or Homo sapiens and early dogs? Did they begin to consort while hunting out on the open savannahs, or sitting around campsites? Did the contact start in Asia or Africa? Having made some inquiries I still have no idea, but I refer the inquiring reader to Google.

Based on what I've read and on what I've seen of dogs, I tend to imagine a primal scene in which predecessors of ours sit around a fire outside their cave. The males look a touch like John Howard; the females, Gina Rinehart. When "John" slings a stripped bone aside the group is at first alarmed, then intrigued to see a wolfish creature slink from the undergrowth, make eye contact with them, grab the bone and dart off into the darkness. That eye contact strikes a chord, so that when the wolfish creature returns next night, and then subsequently with one or two other members of the pack, "Gina," "John," et al., are quite pleased to see them, the more so when they chase predators away from the campsite, dispose of human waste (including turds), and seem keen to make emotional connections.

There is a powerful sense of affinity on both sides. The wolves share the cave with our forebears, their warmth welcome on cold nights, their acute senses a source of security when nocturnal prowlers come in search of food, and if food becomes really scarce "man's best friend" becomes man's next meal.

That inaugurating moment of eye contact now expands into a repertoire of cross-species communication: the "humans" learn to read the pricking ears of the canines for signs of danger or opportunity and to see in their mobile faces emotions that resemble their own. The "wolf-dogs" seem likewise to be able to read human faces; even, after long contact, to interpret the movements of those eyes which, unlike theirs, have large white surrounds (*sclera*). Each learns to read aspects that the other has—canines learn to read hands; "humans" to read tails.

Now supportive cohabitation becomes full-blown collaboration as they learn to hunt together—dogs tracking prey by scent and sound indiscernible to humans and pursuing quarry for longer than they can; "humans" providing spears and high-order communication through language; dogs reading human eye movements and hand signals when vocal messages would mar the hunt.

Evolution likes what it sees: each species helps keep the other secure and fed, and the early wolves that frequent the camp site tend to be a self-selecting bunch. Their genes, which incline them to human contact, are reinforced through breeding with others who are similarly inclined. After eons of prehistoric contact, domestication and strategic breeding start up, shaping even a mutt like Leo into an organic assortment of recognizably modern breeds—labrador, kelpie, perhaps spaniel, and who knows what else. If Issy's long wolfish snout and sleek-slung body recalled his archaic origins, Leo looked more the modern rounded-snout domestic mongrel—until you peered down that primordial white stripe into those almond-brown-flecked eyes.

"Domestication"—is this the right word? I'm with those who think not, who doubt the picture that has "wild" animals coming into contact with more socially advanced "humans" and trading the laws of the jungle for those of the hearth. A persuasive article quotes Jane Goodall, famed observer of chimpanzees:

> Dogs have been domesticated for a very long time. They have descended from wolves who were pack animals. They survive as a result of teamwork. They hunt together, den together, raise pups together. This ancient social order has been helpful in the domestication of the dog. Chimpanzees are individualists. They are boisterous and volatile in the wild. They are always on the lookout for opportunities to get the better of each other. They are not pack animals …
> It is not related to intelligence, but the desire to help, to be obedient, to gain our approval.

Given that we have about 96 percent genetic overlap with chimps, it could be that "wolves" played a significant part in "domesticating" us; that "wildness" was by no means all on their side. Issy's vigils beside Maddie's cot, and Leo's beside Elliot's seven years later, suggest that in social and moral terms co-evolution was mutually beneficial, as was Leo's ability to settle seamlessly into a human family. Wolves are far more likely to accept outsiders than chimpanzees. (Recent genetic analysis reveals more genome overlap between canine and human than previously suspected.)

Stories, including biographies, help humans make sense of and, indeed, celebrate the almost mystical compatibility between humans and dogs. From early on, Leo stories started to proliferate.

Maddie remembers the look of mortified bewilderment on that sensitive white-lined black face when she, at four, dissolved into tears and shouted: "*No Leo! Bad dog!*" after he'd bitten the nobbly brown bulb clean off the end of the snout of Wilbur, her beloved soft-toy polar bear. He was so abashed that I was sure he'd never harass that arctic snout again. But no sooner was it sewn, tooth-scoured and disfigured, back on, than it disappeared again—and again, until, some years later, the long-lost appendage was found on top of the refrigerator as removalists were loading us up to move a couple of suburbs away to a bigger house.

It was from this new house that Ben set out for high school each morning, his plastic West Coast Eagles football club alarm clock set to help this heavy sleeper rise on time. When the alarm failed to sound one morning and he was late for school, Diane, before rushing to work, dashed off a note: "Dear Teacher, Please excuse Ben for being late today. The dog ate his alarm clock." And indeed he had, more or less. Months later, when I gave a talk at the school, Ben's English teacher conducted me to the noticeboard in the staffroom. There, pinned in a prominent position, was Diane's note.

From the moment I saw his face again at Pam's door, I felt an overwhelming protectiveness toward this little dog, who in his brief life had been lost in the mountains, rescued from execution in a pound, had gained and lost a pack, and gained it again. Though never having been taught about roads, he learnt fast to accompany me on long suburban walks. He was generally on his leash, but sometimes where traffic was thin I'd untether him, watching warily as he rummaged, sniffed, and trotted about. On one such occasion he'd scent-meandered fifty yards away. I watched him muzzle about in the front garden of a clapboard cottage and then unaccountably trot into the middle of a road. A young man with wild blond curly hair, one hand on the steering wheel of his van, the other holding a pie, sped toward the unseen pooch. Quite unaware of the danger, the little dog stepped for no apparent reason a few paces to his right. I stood helpless as the van missed him by an inch. Perhaps indeed the little guy's luck was in, but from then on I felt like the Jewish dog owner who knocks up a poster featuring a large photo of the pet, with the headline NOT LOST YET, and distributes it about the neighborhood.

One Sunday afternoon we gathered with other families by the Yarra River for a fund-raising picnic for Ben's school's rowing club. We were feet from the moody brown current, Leo sniffing about—I thought—at nearby trees, when a loud splash told us that he'd taken to the water. In those days the Yarra was so polluted we'd never have swum in it, and we'd occasionally hear stories of people being carried downstream, even drowned, by deceptively swift silt-freighted currents swollen by winter rain. Could this current carry the little dog away? Would the kids and I have to watch him, yowling pitifully, being sucked under? Or would his swimming instinct be strong enough to get him to safety? I didn't know, but after a few seconds of what seemed like lucid assessment, I dove, a very poor swimmer, fully clothed, into those toxic waters, grabbed Leo by the collar and drew him back to the bank.

Maddie, awestruck by my heroics, cried out, "Yay Dad!"

Diane was less impressed: "Shiiiiit! Poor Ben! Other families saw that!"

Whether this was Leo's first experience of swimming is not known, but his next aquatic encounter took place some months later at the coastal town of Point Lonsdale. On this calm summer morning, people dipped and sunned, or sipped and read papers at nearby coffee shops—one of them featuring a sloping concrete sitting-out area, just across the road from the sand.

Dog-loving friends had loaned us their holiday house and said Leo was welcome. When we—parents, Maddie, Maddie's friend Alex, and dog—arrived mid-morning I realized that we hadn't packed any dog food, so I purchased a large packet of the dry variety at the local milk bar. Not noticing that the food—small hard bone-shaped biscuits—was meant to be served as a sort of soup with warm water, I tipped a pile into a bowl. Leo scarcely paused to chew, virtually inhaling the stuff. We then adjourned to the beach, letting him off the leash when we reached the sand. He darted off immediately, having seen a black labrador at the water's edge, and proceeded to hurtle about the beach with an abandon, a *joie de vivre*, that I could only marvel at. The Black Dog—as Churchill called his depressions—had been with me for a few weeks and had followed me to the coast like a stowaway, the putrid feeling of gloom clinging to me even as we set foot on the sand. How odd, I've often thought, that depression has been long likened to one of the most exuberant species we humans ever get to know. Leo's beach romp did wonders for my mood.

⸺ ✿ ⸺

There's a strange photo of me in the *faux* Victorian brick home for which we departed the Edwardian clapboard, taken by I know not whom: I'm lying on my left side on a towel spread over the carpet in the formal living room at the front of the house. My head is resting on two pillows; my left arm is extended straight from my shoulder, my middle finger touches the nose of our cat of the time, Eppie, as if conducting life into her. Leo's black head rests, eyes open, in profile on my upper arm, his back against my stomach. That middle finger, faintly reminiscent of Michelangelo, could not be more misleading: the rest of me looks limp, defeated and lifeless, far less likely to give a yelp than my canine companion. I recoil now from the strange, self-indulgent oddity of the image and from reminders of the gloom that so often sought comfort in the pets.

Mark Doty writes of his "hour of lead" on the Staten Island Ferry. He has lost his partner, Wally, to AIDS and his beloved old dog, Beau, is now terminally ill. He is momentarily tempted to jump overboard, taking the ailing pooch to death with him. "The narcissism of depression," he writes, "is a hole with very deep sides." And of Beau:

> It was only the trusting silent fellow at my feet, who kept looking down into the racing wake through the small hole at the base of the ferry

railing—it was that trust, that day, that kept me in the world.

⸰⸰⸰

In due course, the late morning sun and his lunatic exertion started to take their toll on the dog. Puffed and parched, I saw him wading in the shallows, taking gargantuan gulps of saltwater. Fearing that this might not be good for him I jogged over, returned him to his leash, and led him up the beach to the coffee shop across the road. I tethered Leo at the high end of the sloping concrete floor, went inside with the others to place our orders, then returned to find a table.

Alas, my concerns about the dog's saltwater intake had not been not misplaced. He had disgorged gallons of the stuff in a sort of stew. The biscuit bones, much enlarged by their liquid encounter, oozed and glinted in the sun. A sensation of rising embarrassment clutched at my chest, but was soon displaced by a more immediate and pragmatic concern: the stew was making its way down the concrete slope directly toward a woman of early middle age who was contentedly sipping her coffee and reading the weekend papers.

It was clear to me that, so to speak, I needed to get ahead of the curve; so, leaving Diane to deal with a traumatized waiter, I strode in the most gallant manner I could muster down the slope and addressed the woman: "Excuse me. I'm very sorry to interrupt your coffee in the sun, but you'll understand in a moment why I find it necessary to do so."

The look she gave me as she lifted her eyes from the

newspaper was one of quizzical but friendly surprise, a hint of disdain perhaps politely held in reserve.

Conscious that things would soon come to a head—or rather a foot—I continued, this time gesturing in Leo's direction: "This is so absurd, so embarrassing, that I hardly have words for it, but the fact is that our young dog up there got so hot and excited being at the beach for the first time that he drank a lot of sea water and brought his breakfast up and I'm terribly embarrassed and sorry to say that it is quite literally headed your way."

She looked up, her eyes apparently transfixed by the inexorable alien encroachment. She seemed to hold that pose for several minutes. When her eyes resumed contact with mine her expression resembled that of the hygiene inspector in *Fawlty Towers* in the episode where a rat scuttles across his tray of cheese and biscuits in the hotel dining room.

The moment was so far off the chart that my feelings hardly knew which way to turn. A great wave of shame was on the way, but for the moment I was numb, save for the pressing awareness that something needed to be *done*.

Presently, the woman seemed to blink herself free of her stupor, her eyes flickering back into focus. "Goodness! So it is! How very funny!" she said. And then: "Don't worry. These things happen. It's not a problem."

"Would you like to sit inside while we restore order?"

"No need," she said, "but perhaps you could help me move the table?"

And so, perhaps a minute before the stew would have met that imperturbable woman's morning tea, we relocated her to the outer edge of the concrete where, to my relieved astonishment, she resumed her coffee and papers as if nothing had happened.

The waiter was equally keen to foster the impression that nothing had happened. After deftly assisting me to clear the concrete, he kindly fetched Leo a bowl of fresh water. We parked ourselves at a nearby table, tied Leo's lead to a leg of my chair, and sat waiting for our morning tea, as if nothing had happened.

When our coffee and ice creams arrived, Maddie gaily announced, "I'm going to give Leo a little bit of my ice cream to fill his tummy up again."

"*Don't you dare!*" growled her parents in unison.

⁂

Mark Doty recalls:

> A windy winter day in one of those same salt marshes when we hiked out on the path to scatter Wally's ashes, and Wally's mother threw into the water a single long-stemmed rose, and Beau kept deciding to fetch it back—over and over again, shivering, the pale skin under his strawberry blond growing blue in the cold.

⁂

The narrative now segues from the beach to Beech Street – a transition based on nothing more than the affinities between these two words. So lazy a narrative link might scandalize the protocols of human biography, but one of the pleasures of the canine kind is that ramshackle, whiffy approximation is so deeply *apropos*. Regardless of our cultured refinements, narrative and other, the dogs, as Auden remarks, "go on with their doggy life."

Why the street was called Beech I have no idea, because there wasn't a beech tree in sight. The road was lined by dismal plane trees that looked like broccoli, a particularly desultory one being sunk in the nature strip in front of our new house. We brought baby Elliot home to this abode and Leo kept an eye on the cot, just as Issy had done for Maddie.

Maddie spent countless hours on a trampoline on our large downward-sloping back lawn. Whenever she left the house she'd call out "Tramp boy!" and Leo would come bounding to the back door. If he got to the door before Maddie he'd rise on his hind legs, press the lever-shaped handle down, and let himself out. Witnessing this feat, my dog-loving friend and Shakespeare scholar, John Gillies, christened Leo the Tool-Using Dog.

Under the trampoline lay an assortment of marrowbones in various stages of filth, ravishment and decomposition. As Leo chomped, Maddie would bounce, so that if he happened to be standing up as her mesh-depressing feet reached their nadir, her soles would come within inches of his head. This spectacle could be seen at various times of the day and night, and not just from our back veranda.

Next door lived the novelist, biologist, and biographer, Sally Morrison. Sal was well acquainted with the Black Dog – with our Leo, with her loquacious black (now graying) schnoodle, Wanda, and with the Churchillian disorder to which we were both prone. A comedic exotic of the suburbs, she'd tell how, when sitting in her back garden beside her rotary clothesline named "Janet" (after Janet Howard, the wife of the conservative prime minister of the time), she would see Maddie's dark hair rise above the fence line as the girl approached the zenith of her bounce, and then drop again, like a fuzzy setting sun. From the small apartment she had built in the pitched roof of her house when her son and daughter-in-law had moved in below, Sal had a bird's-eye view of our back garden, including the strewn marrow bones, which she christened the Bone Library. This was fitting: Leo had a studious side and often attended my tutorials, greeting each student as they entered my office and doing wonders for class atmosphere.

Sally became the first chronicler of Leo's life. For Maddie's eighth birthday she wrote the first of three volumes, comprising photographs and typed captions, recounting the engagement and wedding of King Leo and Queen Wanda and then the coronation of the royal couple. The volumes—*The Belligan-Tumpster-Fattigan-Fester Wedding*; *King Leo & Saint Wanda*; and *The Coronation*—were fun with a purpose: Sally knew that that Maddie was finding it hard to adjust to Elliot and that nothing was so likely to console her as a narrative of her beloved "tramp" friend. For good measure, Sally gave the young female protagonist (named Maddie) a title that reconfirmed her shaken centrality in her universe: Maddie was "The Sister-in-charge of-everything." Leo was the King of Kennelvania, and Wanda, St Wanda of St Glitter Spots. Dog snaps, including one of Leo on his back in the grass "displaying the Crown Jewels," are interspersed with languid shots of Maddie, denim skirt, long hair and bare feet, "asking God whether she should become a supermodel," "demonstrating the superiority of her knees to a breathless world," and so on. Photos recall that the wedding, both dogs bedecked in ribbons and the odd patch of glitter, and feasting on liver treats, was a grand affair.

—— ∞ ——

If a dog's luck is in and it is adopted by a family like ours, it lives at the greatest imaginable remove from Darwinian Nature. There will be lonely times suffused with the peculiarly acute separation anxiety that dogs experience when their human family is away (strikingly pairs of dogs feel this just as acutely as solo ones, despite having one another's company), occasional encounters with aggressive pets in parks, the odd clip over the snout for distributing kitchen refuse around the house; but on the whole, park-studded suburbia with a vet nearby is a marvelous invention for dogs—and for humans.

Still, that propensity to anxiety seems to me one of the deepest commonalities between the species: we see and feel it in them; they see and feel it in us. Doty conceives of a human being and companion dog as "one extended consciousness, reaching out in all directions." Would a dog be less anxious if it had language that allowed us better to explain how and why we orchestrate their lives? In some ways, yes; but if language was accompanied—as it would presumably be—by vastly augmented intellectual powers, perhaps not. To know more is to see a great deal more to worry about.

Anxiety, that current that runs through the two species, often flares across species divide. Mine spikes when Leo wanders unaccountably into the middle of a road. The greater care that I exercise thereafter aids his chances of survival. An unaccountable change in Leo's human environment causes canine anxiety, which he registers in a distinctively doggy way …

During the Beech Street years my work obsession would drive my study from one room in the house to another—more space for books, a better view, better ambience for concentration, whatever—sometimes to the detriment of the house's agreeable flow and the rhythms of family life. One move was apparently particularly disconcerting to Leo because he would return to what had been my study where he often snoozed beside me as I wrote, see unfamiliar furniture, and leave vast puddles in the white carpet. Dog owners live in their pets' piddly worlds without perhaps quite getting the protocols of bladder-emptying on trees, posts, signs, human accouterments. We get to share their mysterious urine-mapped universe happily enough in parks—less so indoors.

Our local vet, a stolid, kind, efficient man by the name of Ken Kelly, having eliminated bladder trouble and other organic malfunctions as possible causes, explained that Leo, mildly unhinged by the changing topography of the house, was perhaps re-marking his territory. But the frequency and fecundity of his deposits indicated the presence of an unusually high level of anxiety, even in this highly strung dog.

"What can be done about anxiety in dogs?" I asked. "Tranquilizers?"

"In cases like this we recommend Prozac," Ken said. "It's more effective and has fewer side-effects."

"*Really?*"

"Yes," he said. "Specially formulated for dogs, of course."

And so the Black Dog commenced a two-month course of Prozac, one embedded each morning in a dollop of liverwurst.

The puddles had ceased altogether by the time I tipped the final pill from its plastic vial. Sal and I, votaries of the "Happy Pill's" mysterious powers, raised glasses to Ken's psychiatric acumen.

Now time passed, as it is inclined to do, though even after decades of cohabitation with canines it's impossible to know how the passing of time feels to a dog. Do they, for instance, register watershed moments, as when the portly and arthritic Leo found that, all of a sudden, he could no longer jump up onto our bed unassisted? Did he think the canine equivalent of "*Shit!* I used to be able to do that without a stool! *What's* going on?"; or "*Jesus*, I'm getting old! Wonder how much longer I've got?"

Perhaps time merely passes for them, as it often does for us, as a mute continuum, a featureless in-between filler, dotted for them by sleep, our absences, meals, play, anxious-making visits to the vet and much that we would regard as merely incidental—the *rrruummm!* of the postman's motorbike.

For those prone to the Black Dog, in-between time spells danger. Bereft of self-defining or affirming deeds, these drab expanses are breeding grounds for worry, self-dismay and the fashioning of gloomy narrative scenarios. Dogs, sources of sweet momentary pleasure for their owners, and the simple, fascinating delights of sharing life with another species, seem fashioned equally for momentary excitement and simply *being* in the in-between.

Leo, like Issy, found endless delight in tennis balls, and so old routines were repeated, now with a slurpy old steel-framed racquet, on a sports oval not far away. But it was repetition with variation: nature, breeding or whatever, had equipped Leo with the pursuit reflex but not the retrieval one. He'd thunder after the ball then stand chewing it, head rocking from side to side, as if preparing to swallow. No amount of whistling, clapping or calling would summon him to where I stood, and if I approached him the game would switch to "catch me if you can." The solution was to take two balls to the park and to hit one while Leo was chewing the other, collect the one he'd just dropped in favor of the one I'd just hit, and so on, until fatigue set in and I could pocket one ball then wrench the other from panting jaws.

Maddie and I used to play tennis on clay courts a couple of streets away. The first time we took Leo with us I let him off the leash, sat him at the back of the court, and commanded him to "*stay there!*" But it was hopeless—he'd fly after each ball, often skidding at high speed into the net. He was sweetly incensed when we tethered him to a tree outside the court.

———

Between our house and Sally's stood a fine old magnolia tree, and in the tree lived several generations of possums. We'd all known the possums from their roof-scuttlings and blood-curdling nocturnal snarls; but when Sal moved to the apartment at the top of her house, becoming, as we said, the "Madwoman in the Attic," she found herself living at eye level with these exquisite but wary creatures. Her way across this species divide was to lay a trail of cheese and apple bits along the balustrade of her veranda. Once night had fallen, a procession of possums of all ages—old and motley, young and sleek, mothers with babes in pouch or clinging to their undersides—would make its dainty way along the wooden beams, each pausing to lift food in delicate front claws and nibble warily before moving on. I'd often take the kids up there before dusk to witness this Brothers Grimm-like parade. Leo would come too, but he and Wanda had to watch the proceedings whiningly behind glass doors.

As night was falling, Sal would serve biscuits, juice, lemonade and tea, the dogs darting off after biscuit bits that were flung across her small living room, or schmoozing with us on the sofas. One night I saw Sally's hand pause and probe the flesh to the left of Leo's snout.

"Come and feel this," she said to me.

Dogs become so lumpy and bumpy as they age that I'd have thought nothing of the small lump under my fingertips, but the biologist in Sal suggested that Ken Kelly should have a look at it. He biopsied the lump and advised that it was a "mast cell carcinoma"—not a deadly cancer but one that could spread to the eye socket and beyond if it weren't completely removed. To do so he would have to take a margin of the surrounding healthy tissue. It wouldn't be a problem, he said, but because of its location that side of Leo's face would be pinched and he'd have the look of "a permanent snarl."

Leo—a permanent snarl! It seemed so absurdly out of character. And wouldn't he terrify neighborhood kids who didn't know that the snarl wasn't really his?

The lampshade he had to wear over his head after the operation to keep him from scratching the wound caused its fair share of terror, alarmed kids in parks skedaddling as the lampshade on legs trotted unsuspectingly toward them. And he did sport an oddly immobile, unconvincing snarl for many months after the operation, like a botoxed heartthrob who's seen better days. But gradually the snarl subsided and that benign face returned almost to normal. We reckoned that Leo was to be congratulated on devoting himself so assiduously to his facial exercises.

Two of the operation's effects were, however, permanent. That muzzle stripe, hitherto a little bolt of white lightning shot from those wolfish eyes right to the end of his snout, now meandered to the left, fanning out into a diffuse white-gray patch on his left cheek before sinking from view. And from then on the dog would have to be on steroids to inhibit recurrence of the tumor. This, Ken explained, would make him ravenously hungry. He suggested that I liberally augment Leo's food with raw carrot pieces—a measure he welcomed as warmly as any horse would have done.

However, as hunger sharpened his scavenging skills in park barbeque areas, shopping strips, and bins, his girth steadily expanded. The kids and I fell about laughing when one day we saw him trying to retard his own rapid progress down a steep hill, frantically rotating his tail like the flapping parachute behind a passenger jet as it touches down. In family lore he became The Barrel on Toothpicks, a creature of a sedate, gently rollicking gait to whom a tennis ball was a destination rather than a quarry.

As he aged, time visibly crept over him—the white frill about his jaw edging its way up his face to within an inch of his eyes, a milky film settling on his corneas. The in-between times seemed to expand too, as he did less, slept longer, took shorter walks. Though more securely embedded than ever with the family he adored, his ever-present anxiety could still flare, especially when he was left alone.

What did he make of the big changes that occurred now and then? Of things less gradual than the stealth of advancing age? What was he thinking when he'd hear Eppie, our very old cat and his beloved sibling, mewing her strange demented mew on the hallway stairs, and he'd walk up to her, touching her nose with his, calming the disoriented creature? When she died he clearly missed her, checking her former haunts, looking up at me in what seemed like pained puzzlement.

When a few weeks later we brought the kitten Peanut home, we orchestrated the first encounter between cat and dog in the family room, Maddie with Leo on her lap in one chair, Peanut on my lap in another. When he set eyes on the new arrival Leo quietly yowled in a way that we'd never heard before and never heard again. Was he objecting to a new arrival in the pack? Or welcoming her? Did he know that Peanut's advent meant that Eppie was gone forever? Maddie and I still talk of this moment. That yowl, whatever it was, moved us like a human *cri de coeur*, so complex in its pain, its perplexity, so richly aware, even though we could only guess at what it meant.

—◆—

Dogs bring death as well as delight into our lives. Vonnegut might have referred to the dogs we have lost, not just to those we have "known." The demise of a dog is often a child's first experience of death. To live with a dog is to feel a kind of sadness—that animals who commit with such wholehearted, intelligent joy to life will only have it for a few fleeting years. Though we assess that brevity relative to human life spans, the sadness is perhaps about us as well as them; we know all too well that in the vast scheme of things our lives are absurdly fleeting as well, a momentary flicker of a match in a darkened room. Doty writes of dogs' "relationship to time":

Because dogs do not live as long as we do, they

seem to travel a faster curve than human beings, flaring into being, then fading away while we watch. An animal's life is for us a theater, in which we may see the forces of time and mortality played out in a form smaller than our own bodies, and more swiftly. An Aurora Borealis Theater?

This too endows their lives with biographical import.

Perhaps, as the psychiatrist Irvin D. Yalom argues in *Staring at the Sun*, because we live with the knowledge of death the Black Dog appears in many human lives, often making an appearance among dog lovers when we know, as the dog perhaps does not, that the pet has little time left.

All of this was in the air when I took the now grizzled and somewhat rickety Leo for his annual check-up. Ken was pleased to report that the facial tumor had not recurred but the probing fingers of his right hand reached the dog's throat and paused.

"Hello. Something here. Have you noticed this?"

I placed my hand there. No, I hadn't noticed it, which was surprising given that there was a lump the size of a small orange in the vicinity of Leo's larynx.

"Is it likely to be bad?" I asked.

"Well, it's unlikely to be good but we can't be sure until we see the pathology. There's no real point in a biopsy because if we don't remove this thing soon he won't be able to swallow. We'll need to move fast."

Within a few days of the operation I called back to get the pathology results. Ken had been unable to remove the entire, apparently entangled, tumor and had prepared me for gloomy news.

"Mr. Freadman, I'm afraid that it's as I thought. The tumor is ultra-nasty. One of the worst. The operation will give Leo some relief but he doesn't have much time left."

"What would you predict?"

"You can never be sure because cancer by its very nature doesn't play by the rules. But I wouldn't be expecting more than about six weeks."

I stopped off in a park on the way home to let the gloom settle. It wasn't the searing gloom you might feel about a close family member or friend. Leo was, after all, a dog, and we know that dogs' lives are short. What I felt was a kind of enervation at having the brevity of these beautiful creatures' lives confirmed again, at the prospect of family distress, at the thought of renewing eye contact with that trusting creature now that this imbalance of power and knowledge had entered our relationship—my knowing he was doomed, he presumably having no idea—and preparing for weeks or months of waiting for him to die. I could feel depression closing in. The Black Dog.

The kids were less devastated than I had feared.

"Oh … isn't there anything they can do?"

"Poor Leo—he's such a sweet man …"

But there was a resilience in those kiddie souls that had long departed mine—if indeed it had ever been there.

"I know," said Maddie. "Let's get another dog to keep Leo happy, and when Leo dies we won't feel so sad because we'll still have a dog."

"Yeah," said Ben, "a transition pup!"

I didn't much like the idea but soon they were googling breeds, looking forward to another dog, excitedly imagining a future as I was dreading the denouement.

They settled on a schnoodle—a cross between a schnauzer and poodle—and located a breeder in a light-industrial area half an hour away. When we pulled up at a suburban house in large dusty grounds cluttered with cages and fenced-in areas, a man in football shorts and a faded aqua t-shirt walked out to greet us.

"G'day. I'm Merv. Did youse come for a cuppa, a cold one, or are youse interested in a dog?"

Since he had known that we would be arriving at about that time in the hope of buying a schnoodle, this was a species of Australian rhetorical question, albeit more familiar to me than to the rest of the slightly bemused family.

Merv led us to a cage containing a mother and six very young and beautiful schnoodle puppies. Some were romping; others were asleep; perhaps one was feeding. I think we were all feeling charmed and awed and a little apprehensive about breaking up this serene family unit when loud screeching overhead shattered the silence.

"Bloody bird!" huffed Merv as a huge, shiny black crow with blazing eyes touched down on the fence railing a few feet away.

"Hang on a minute, will youse?" said Merv, remonstrating affectionately with the bird then walking to a hut which housed a refrigerator. He removed a large can of Chum dog food from the fridge, picked up a tablespoon from a nearby bench, gouged an apple-sized chunk out of the can and held it out to the bird. It devoured the Chum with rapacious speed, seeming to nod rapidly at Merv as it ate.

"A pain in the arse, that bloody bird!" Merv blustered, gazing up almost lovingly as the stunning creature took flight, perhaps to predate on cans of Chum in the wild.

There were no reasonable grounds upon which to choose one of the puppies above any of the others but we settled on one that seemed notably relaxed, paid Merv a handsome sum, and headed home with the kids nursing the puppy in the back seat. Here was further evidence of profound evolutionary kinship between the species: far from being distressed by his removal from the pack, the pup slept peacefully on Maddie's lap all the way home. Later, though, Maddie had to calm him by wrapping him in a blanket with a clock ticking in imitation of a mother's heart, as he slept on her bed.

Maddie christened the little curly-haired grayish-black dog "Haggis," perhaps in part because of his Scots ancestry. He was cavortingly flawless, despite—to our sorrow—having had his tail lopped during the first day of his life, and his effect on the ailing Leo was remarkable. The old dog brightened up, his fur regained its former sheen; he played gently and protectively with the pup, and they settled into a lovely relationship, part-partners and part mentor and protégé. Expected to die within six weeks, Leo lived another eighteen months. A chuck under the chin was now a chuck under the tumor; but we all got used to that.

The beach shack we bought at Blairgowrie in 2005 when Leo was fourteen years old bore his imprint until we re-did the floors many years later. After several acclimatizing visits we thought it safe to leave him there alone while we went out to dinner, but in a frantic fit of desertion anxiety he burrowed through the carpet at the base of the front door and left deep gouge marks in the chipboard beneath.

But he came quickly to associate the coast with a dog beach ten minutes away by car. We never walked the four kilometers, preferring to save our energy for the tranquil stretch of beach aproned on one side by the masts of yachts in the local marina, and for the euphoric conviviality of that butt-sniffing, hurtling, gallivanting and splashing dog nirvana. Leo loved the place, as later did Haggis, who hurtled with the best of them while the arthritic Leo waddled sedately along the foreshore.

Some local residents who did not love dogs insisted that their council police the dog beach assiduously. In the summer holiday season off-leash hours didn't begin until 7 p.m., so I'd often take the pooches for a walk on the cusp of dusk. I had to watch the scatty Haggis like a hawk because he liked to sprint off into the bush and the caravan parks that nestled between highway and beach. Leo would seldom plod beyond my field of vision.

On one occasion, I had to leave the beach to retrieve Haggis from a barbeque in the caravan park. When I got back I looked for Leo but couldn't see him. I assumed that he was nuzzling about in nearby bushes and that he would appear when summoned by the usual whistling and clapping. But he did not.

I walked on—and back—not feeling too bothered, keeping my faithful old companion, anxiety, at bay. But still no Leo. Old habits started to cut in—mounting waves of alarm bearing awful scenarios: a snakebite in the bushes; a heart attack like Issy's. Could he have drowned, found his way onto the highway and been run over, fallen into sadistic hands?

The family drove down to join the search, now by torchlight, while I scanned the nearby area in my car. It was a warm moonlit night and cars swished past on the wide highway with their high beams momentarily dimmed. I drove up the beach side of the road, getting out every few hundred yards to clap and call and then, having traveled further than Leo could have walked in that time, turned back and did the same thing on the other side, calling and clapping into front gardens, pathways and empty lots. Nothing.

I circled back, thinking he must be in one of the camping areas or small patches of parkland that border the beach. As I approached each of these I swerved off the road into the darkness, the headlights catching the incandescent tips of teenagers' cigarettes, the luminous eyes of campers' dogs, a fox gliding into the undergrowth, the moonlit ripples on the water glimpsed between timber beach boxes. The car blundered over rocks, bumped to earth after scaling mounds, juddered through ditches. I was driving like a lunatic, and as I veered out of each enclave of night and into the next I felt a strange abandon, my habitual dread of being unsafe misting off into the dark, the only fear now the fear for Leo.

I returned to the beach and was about to begin trudging its length again when the phone rang. It was the family. They'd driven back to a shopping center on the highway, a kilometer from the house, waiting to hear from me.

Leo knew this place, and there, outside the kids' favorite burger shop, he was waiting for us. The venerable, arthritic, milky-eyed old chap had walked kilometers in the dark through unfamiliar territory to re-join his pack.

———

Leo's lump persisted without apparent change and he remained ravenously hungry. Things seemed completely stable until, shortly before I was due to make a preliminary visit to Hong Kong where I had accepted an academic position, he started to make a quiet tick-like gagging noise. Unsure what it might portend, Ken referred me to Phil, an unassuming and conscientious specialist in animal oncology. After a thorough examination, Phil told me that while cancer is unpredictable, he did not think that Leo would fall seriously ill during the six weeks I planned to be away, though he did not have long to live. And so I went.

The kids started lobbying for another transition pup, but we desisted because it would be too much to take two dogs to Hong Kong.

I remember well—or has memory embellished it?— the last time I patted Leo, on the gray slate hallway of our house, before leaving for the airport. I don't think I thought that I might not see him again, because I had been reassured by the specialist; but perhaps my native pessimism caused me to pause and stroke his head with particular lingering tenderness. Perhaps the uncanny creature sensed something too, because his grizzled, slightly lopsided loving look seemed almost mournful. I don't know.

—⁂—

Within hours of my arrival in Hong Kong the family rang to say that Leo had gone into a decline. He was lying on Maddie's bed almost unable to move and barely bothering to eat. The kids were taking his food and water to him. Diane took him to Phil, who said that there had been a sharp downturn in his condition and that he should be monitored carefully. Would he last until I got back? He did not know.

Hong Kong, that extraordinary assortment of East and West now apprehensively "handed back" to mainland China, promised an exciting new phase in our lives. But that little dog was constantly on my mind as I traveled about in cheap taxis and clattering minibuses. The family reported that he was losing weight, losing interest in them and in Haggis, and soiling the blanket he was lying on. I thought about flying back, but even to me that seemed excessive. Perhaps he would last another few weeks. I thought of Issy who had passed into a coma in that cage in Perth and how bitterly I had regretted that. But Leo was at home with the family and was apparently in no discomfort. I had things that needed doing in Hong Kong. So I stayed.

A few days later Diane rang to say that Leo had "turned his face to the wall." He had lost all interest in life and seemed to want to die. She rang Phil who said Leo had come to the end and that Diane should bring him to the surgery to be euthanized.

Sai Kung is an exquisite fishing village on the northeast coast of Hong Kong's New Territories. Though one of the most dog-friendly parts of often dog-averse Hong Kong, the endless rows of marine animals in tanks outside seafood restaurants on the quay are a reminder of the Darwinian scheme of things, not least, in some parts of China, for dogs.

I'd been looking at apartments with views of the beautiful island-girded bay and was on a minibus on a dusty road in Man On Shan, a nearby town, when a text arrived from Elliot: "Leo has gone. The vet put him to sleep." I got out of the bus and phoned the family.

Diane had carried the unprotesting animal, now weighing no more than an overcoat, to Phil and had watched as the green fluid passed into his veins and took him away in an instant at the ripe age of fifteen. Not normally given to tears, she'd cried all the way home. I felt empty.

The transition-pup lobby eventually got its way. Haggis was mourning and moping—the black dog's version of the human affliction that goes by that name—and so were the kids. On the way back from her basketball training Maddie saw a pet shop, and with Elliot's support persuaded Diane to stop. There she bonded instantly with a little Australian wirehair terrier, the last of the litter in the cage. There were four in the car on the way home and the new arrival, who would soon accompany Haggis to Hong Kong, was christened McDuff.

Two weeks later, scuttling paws scampered to the front door to greet me. Haggis leapt; McDuff yapped and scrabbled. The kids followed, carrying a clumsily embossed mahogany wooden box. Leo's ashes.

Nine

Renata

Shall you comprehend your mother, or only blame her?

—George Eliot, *Daniel Deronda*

… a man to feel touched in the contemplation of.

—Charles Dickens, *David Copperfield*

Some of us, if we're lucky, meet someone early in life who seems to get us in a way we don't yet get ourselves, and whose confidence in us helps defuse the self-doubt, even self-despair, that might threaten our ability to fashion a good life. I met Renata at a time when I felt vulnerable, unsure, sometimes panicky, and she became a steadying, wise, reassuring and immensely important figure for me. She was both friend and mentor: better still, she was a mentor-friend.

I'd just arrived as an eighteen-year-old foreign student at Brandeis University in Waltham, a twenty-minute drive northwest of Boston. It was 1969, three years after the abolition of the White Australia policy. Having spent most of my life under that magnanimous regime and feeling a touch homesick, I was pleased when a friendly African-American guy tapped on my half-open dormitory room door, came in, and started to chat. Fascinated to hear where I was from, he peppered me with questions about Australia. He also took an interest in the worldly goods I'd brought with me. He seemed particularly taken with my Minolta camera, which he rotated against the light like a jeweler assessing an antique vase, and various knick-knacks I'd acquired during the six-week boat trip to the United States. Spying a shiny plastic wallet and clearly feeling at his ease, he picked it up, opened it, and professed amazement at what he beheld—dollar bills, but with a difference! So anxious was I to please and to demonstrate the breadth of my racial sympathies that I happily explained that these were American dollar traveler's checks purchased in Australia. I even explained how they were used. He seemed genuinely impressed by this information.

We chatted on, the discussion becoming so congenial that I felt I might have made a firm friend on my second day on campus. Presently I had to go to sign up for a student card; he apologized for detaining me, agreed that we must meet again soon, and took his leave.

Two days later, sitting on a grassy rise at a campus orientation function, I made the acquaintance of Mark Maimone, an agile, dark-haired and bearded man of my age, with anxiously amused brown eyes behind black-rimmed glasses. A freshman music major from Long Island, he too was interested to hear that I was Australian, explaining that his mother, an avid reader and a great admirer of Patrick White, had written to the novelist asking whether she might meet him when she visited Sydney with the Long Island Youth Orchestra. I was surprised to hear that the curmudgeonly genius had granted her an audience.

When Mark inquired how I was settling in, I told him that things were going well, the exception being that I'd lost my traveler's checks and had to report to the police in Waltham, and also to a bank, to organize new checks. As it happened, Mark's family had a long history in the area—his maternal grandparents, one of whom was Jewish, had settled in nearby Newtonville when they got out of Germany just before the war—and he himself was living there now with an elderly relative. He offered to drive me to the Waltham town center and help get my problem sorted. I was more than pleased to accept his offer.

The police were in little doubt as to the fate of my traveler's checks: a highly accomplished ring of thieves had been touring many of the area's numerous institutions of higher education, sometimes even loading contraband into a van that cruised the campuses as foot soldiers knocked on doors and surveyed the contents of dormitory rooms. In due course many of the gang were arrested and convicted, including my cordial visitor.

And so a den of thieves helped facilitate two of the great friendships of my life.

⸺⸺

When I met Mark on that rise I was an indulged and self-indulgent young man, driven by inner compulsions and conflicts more powerful than my fragile emotional states could handle. When "up," my aspirational energies and optimism seemed limitless; when "down," I could barely raise a yelp and imagined myself to be of negligible value to the world and quite incapable of holding my own at an elite American university. The American-Australian girlfriend I'd traveled over with had just returned to her native Virginia to start college. For a young man prone to sexual suspicion, a long-distance relationship was a recipe for turmoil. My inner disquiet meant I did not enjoy my own company. I would become acutely lonely when the Americans in my dormitory left campus on weekends and during vacations.

It was fortunate for me that my new acquaintance was somewhat retiring, didn't know many people in Boston and wasn't making many friends on campus, which he generally visited only for classes. The two of us would often band together on weekends, listening to music or an LP of *Monty Python's Flying Circus* that an English foreign student had brought with him. Quite why we were so taken with Monty Python is hard to say. Perhaps Python took the heat out of our fear of failure by lampooning the world on whose terms we yearned to succeed. Or maybe it emboldened our disdain for what seemed to have no worth, thereby affirming our lofty ideals? Whatever it was, our conversations would generally begin, in tones inspired by John Cleese and the "Parrot Sketch," with "*Sir!* I will *not have it!*"—a mode of address that often left fellow students looking a touch bewildered.

No doubt I managed to look suitably mournful when, a few weeks into the semester, the subject of an upcoming vacation arose. Soon after, I was invited to stay with Mark and his family on Long Island, two hundred miles away, during the break. His mother's message, via Mark, was that they were looking forward to welcoming the Australian member of the family, or something to that effect. Much though I appreciated this, I wondered if she might be given to a certain gushy effusiveness that I was encountering a lot on campus.

In due course, Mark's old Saab puttered into the driveway of the family home in Roslyn Harbor. The house, with its sharp-sloping roof and two dormer windows on the first floor, was an unpretentious paraphrase of Dutch-Colonial style. It had a generous front lawn and nestled among towering pine trees at the side and back. As the car pulled in, a white-haired woman in large pastel-colored glasses stepped out of the front door and waved enthusiastically. Not at that stage being a hugger, I was slightly taken aback by the heartiness of her embrace when I climbed out of the car, but I felt instantly at ease as Renata said something like: "Welcome to our Australian cousin! We have been so much looking forward to *meeting* you!"

If her high cheekbones, shapely face and gray-blue eyes suggested that she had been a beauty in her youth, her current appearance—little or no makeup, straight short white hair parted at one side, comfortable clothes in pastel and tweed—was strikingly free of vanity. I was to learn that to Renata, a fashion magazine was a cultural toxin and that time spent shopping fussily for clothes was time squandered. She started each day with a yoga routine, was an inveterate swimmer, and looked lithe and fit. She stood straight: her height a bit above average.

The large living room to the left of the hallway as we entered the house featured a grand piano, a harpsichord, and furniture of Scandinavian inspiration, including a subdued striped sofa with wooden arms. I was surveying this tasteful, orderly space when a door swung open across the hallway releasing great gusts of pipe smoke and football commentary.

"Is he here yet?" boomed a voice.

Confirmation received, a stocky Sicilian-American man emerged. He had brushed-back wavy dark hair, a jowly face and black-rimmed glasses that vastly magnified all that they encircled. He shook my hand, looking me straight in the eye and grinning. Joe Maimone, Mark's father, never tired of pronouncing "Australian" in a variety of absurd accents, so he probably said something like, "So this is the Orstrailyine." Various quips about my country of origin and the dubious company I was keeping at Brandeis followed, and then, without preliminaries, he launched into a joke. Joe told me so many jokes over the years, all of them in multiple iterations, that I'm not sure which one he selected to welcome me into his home but I think it may have been the one about two scouts—one Indian, the other a federal soldier—who, unbeknownst to one another, are inching their way toward each other along opposite sides of a covered wagon, gathering intelligence before a battle. When the soldier hears Indian drums in the distance, he exclaims, "I don't like the sound of that drumming!" The Indian, who is now within hearing range of his counterpart, replies, "I don't like it either, but he's not our regular drummer."

Joe's way of delivering a joke was inimitable. His almond-brown eyes, vastly enlarged by his thick glasses, would peer waveringly off into the distance. A look of watery-eyed bewilderment, such as might possess a man of meager intelligence pondering Einstein's equation, would come over his face. In his thick Bronx accent he seemed likely to fumble a line at any moment, but in fact he almost never stumbled; and as he delivered the punch line he'd throw his head back and laugh uproariously at his own joke, a wheeze cascading into a guttural eruption.

Mark, Jeff (his older brother who had just joined us from his bedroom upstairs), and I fell about laughing. Renata, though clearly amused, had no doubt heard the gag a hundred times before and seemed keen to proceed to weightier things.

"Well, make yourself at home!" shouted Joe, returning to his study.

The house stood on an acre of land, the back lawn disappearing into thick undergrowth beneath the pines and gnarled old apple trees. Renata was to write in her autobiography of her early and abiding love of nature. During her German childhood her family rented a summer house in a:

> very small village amidst green hills, fields and a narrow stream that was a never-ending source of delight for me. I could follow the geese and sit among the blue forget-me-nots, letting the water run over my feet. Small fish were darting between rocks, forever escaping my clumsy fingers. It was good to lie in one of the fenced-in meadows and look up into the clouds, or turn around and watch small insects climb up a blade of grass.

It was typical of her that she'd left the deeper recesses of the Roslyn Harbor back garden uncultivated, so that wildlife could thrive and the boys could share the experience of nature with her.

The other great love of her childhood was music. The grand piano, a Steinway, was one of the few possessions her parents had been able to bring out from Germany. (She was to write an unpublished history of the family centerd upon that grand instrument.) Renata was one of the founders of live classical music performance on Long Island. Upstairs, across the landing from the boys' bedrooms, was her studio where she taught, did organizational work for the Long Island Baroque Ensemble, the Long Island Youth Orchestra and other organizations, and where the boys practiced – Mark the cello, Jeff the flute. Renata and Joe would sing duets, and hold concerts in their living room, as they had in their previous home, and as her parents had in Germany.

Despite my father's great love and knowledge of music, my musical culture is thin. I could never adequately share music with Renata or Mark. And yet, as Mark wrote in his eulogy for Renata in 2005, she and I "hit it off immediately." Indeed I felt marvelously and uncharacteristically relaxed with her from that first day in Roslyn Harbor onwards.

The world dealt the young Renata a complicated, though in some ways privileged, hand. Born in Berlin on 11 June 1917, she was highly intelligent and had a naturally strenuous, retentive, and subtle mind. From her father, Albert Elsberg, an acculturated Jewish-German ophthalmologist from an Orthodox background, she inherited an equable, coping temperament.

Renata's maternal grandfather suffered from acute bipolar disorder, and was cared for by his wife. Their daughter, Renata's mother Maria Huver, inherited this condition but was able to live what appeared from the outside to be a relatively normal life until old age, when dementia finally dashed her fragile hold on reality. As a young woman, Maria formed a tumultuous relationship with a cousin who was a painter, had several abortions during that relationship, and then a failed first marriage with another man. (The cousin later murdered his wife and children and took his own life.) Worn down by decades of living with a mentally ill husband, anxious about money and distressed by her daughter's unstable personal life, Renata's grandmother hanged herself. Her grandfather died in a mental institution.

Maria met Albert and married him around 1914. Renata was born three years later.

From her mother, Renata inherited fine musical gifts. But the musical ambitions of both mother and daughter were to be frustrated. Maria's life story was tragic in this respect also. Her vast vocal talent was ruined by poor early tuition that damaged her vocal chords. She became a highly regarded voice teacher in Berlin and later at the New England Conservatory of Music in Boston, and she drove the talented Renata hard at singing, hoping that her daughter could achieve the success that had been denied her.

A passage in the autobiography about taking singing lessons with her mother typifies the power and sadness with which Renata wrote and spoke about this mother-daughter relationship:

> When I turned sixteen my mother decided that it was time to train my voice. She gave me a

lesson nearly every day. It was great fun at first. For years I had been listening to singing lessons; I already knew many songs and arias from hearing them over and over again. Without being aware, I had already formed definite ideas [about] how to interpret these songs. But first I had to gain technical control over my voice, and there are no short cuts in voice training. It takes time and patience. For my mother this was the perfect opportunity to create the singer who would demonstrate that her method was infallible, and who would enhance her reputation as a teacher.

The human voice is the most sensitive of all musical instruments. Body and mind have to be in harmony, and the least physical or emotional tension will interfere with a smooth tone production ... After the first few corrections and criticisms my muscles would begin to tighten. The tension would spread to my vocal chords and constructive work would become nearly impossible.

Our mother-daughter relationship was already a strained one: I had developed an attitude of passive resistance ...

Because music came laced with maternal mania, Renata could not simply receive it like a gift. In order to become a musician, and indeed to become herself, she had to learn how to live well—a skill that her mother could scarcely master, given the violent fluctuations of her moods.

Renata wrote and spoke often of her attitude of passive

resistance, which she later recognized as an unconscious survival strategy, a form of compartmentalization that served to establish boundaries with a parent who did not "do" boundaries and who would not, probably could not, leave her daughter room to grow:

> Unconsciously I must have closed myself off from her already as a child, sensing that she wanted to direct all my thoughts and actions. I saw how she ruled and subdued my father and I wanted to avoid suffering the same fate. Early on I got into the habit of dealing with conflicts by myself, being outwardly agreeable and diffident. This has been, and still is, difficult for those close to me.

In this situation—exacerbated by being an only child—Renata learnt to cultivate solitude. This skill was to sustain her in many ways but, as she acknowledges here, it could at times complicate family life. Once when I was at dinner at the family home, Joe, who was prone to brief eruptions of Sicilian irritability, accused Renata of being "cold." Renata seemed scarcely to bat an eyelid and the moment soon passed. But it doubtless reflected difficulties in the relationship between these two fond, fine but strikingly different people.

Mark and Renata had a very good relationship. Alike in many ways, they shared the love of music and nature, and a core set of social values. Like any son, Mark could occasionally sound impatient when speaking of his mother, but as mother-son relationships went, this one struck me as being unusually sustaining and straightforward. And yet

Mark's long and superb eulogy for Renata began thus:

> It might seem strange to say at this moment, but
> in many ways, I feel I didn't know my mother
> very well. Perhaps this is because I share some of
> her personality: in particular, a natural reticence
> and reluctance to focus on myself.

In later life, it seems to me, Renata tried—for her
own sake and for those close to her—to make sense of
her solitude and, by so doing, to release herself from that
state into one that was more spontaneous and open, less
self-contained. An important—perhaps crucial—aspect
of this endeavor was the writing of her autobiography, an
activity that is both solitary and a kind of sharing. At age
sixty-eight she wrote *Detours and By-ways: Journey through
a life*, which was never published. In its first paragraph she
explains:

> Daydreams and inner monologues dealing with
> events and unresolved conflicts of the past have
> become more and more insistent of late. They are
> straining my habitual reticence to disclose myself,
> looking for a crack to burst into the open.

What issues from this "crack" is autobiography with a deep
ethical impulse—ethical in the ancient sense of how to
live a good life, including how to "flourish", to fulfill one's
capacities; and ethics understood as a set of moral attitudes
that guide one's life as a social being. Renata wrote that
the Holocaust left her if not quite with survivor guilt, then
with something she called "survivor conscience":

> Perhaps this survivor conscience is responsible

for a restless drive to do something worthwhile with my life. Although who is to judge what is worthwhile and what isn't? I am still possessed by the need to be engaged in projects that affect others beside myself.

She pursued many such projects, her mentoring of my muddled younger self being one of them; she also sought, through writing and other engagements, to diffuse inner impediments to her own flourishing. Her autobiography is perhaps above all a story of gradual emancipation from existential constraints. In *Writing a Woman's Life*, Carolyn Heilbrun cautions against co-opting the language of male triumph—like Sartre's formulation "the history of a liberation"—when writing women's lives. Yet in its own modest way I do think Renata's life is appropriately characterized as a liberation.

As in a Bildungsroman novel the story begins in "passive resistance," a reactive state in which she merely acts in response to various internal and external pressures; gradually and often painfully she learns to read situations, to weigh options, and to make emotionally and rationally discerning decisions. It would be naïve to imagine that this state, which sometimes goes by the name of "individual agency," ever enables anyone to be entirely free. Renata well knew that all lives are limited by circumstantial and temperamental constraints, among others. She deplored crudely individualistic American notions of "personal liberty" and the blandishments of self-help books that promised complete inner freedom. But she believed deeply that each person has a right to flourish and a chance to do so—given reasonable circumstances—if they exercise a degree of discerning authority in their own lives.

Again on the first page of *Detours and By-ways*, she writes:

> The events of my life have been shaped by outside forces and by other people. Relatively late in life I began to assume control and to make deliberate choices. Now I am attempting to find a pattern in the many detours and side roads I have taken over the years.

Looking back, she is amazed and even appalled at how much time on that precious journey was spent in detours and by-ways, often because it took her so long to take charge of its trajectories. She repeatedly describes her earlier self as "passive," "drifting", and her early life impressed upon her the power that outside and internal forces alike could exert: though her family escaped Nazi persecution, her existence, identity and sense of moral order were profoundly shaken by the war. Her mother's illness showed her what devastation could be wrought by unbridled, mercurial psychic energies.

Maria's domineering neediness seems to have complicated Renata's search for personal identity in many ways, and the autobiography is at one level an attempt to answer the question posed to Daniel Deronda by his mother the Princess Halm Eberstein: "Shall you comprehend your mother, or only blame her?" Of her own maternal feelings, this woman who had left him to be raised by others while she pursued her career as an opera singer tells him: "I have not felt exactly what other women feel—or say they feel."

Renata's father, Albert, was a Reform Jew who attended synagogue on High Holy Days, and a committed Zionist. He possessed an unwavering sense of Jewish identity, as did his father. Renata had vivid and haunting childhood memories of "hearing my grandfather's ritual prayers through the wall, in a language I could not understand" during family visits. (She recalls these visits in an unpublished, avowedly fictional narrative, in which, strikingly, the little girl protagonist is called Maria.) Her grandfather was to lose a son and her father a brother in a concentration camp when Renata was in her early twenties.

Her mother, a Christian who professed agnosticism in her rebellious earlier days, became something of a religious zealot in the late 1930s. In one of several disturbingly intrusive and turbulent maternal letters that Renata quotes in *Detours and By-ways*, Maria writes to her about her religious conversion and urges Renata, then nineteen, to follow suit:

> The great inner change did not make my life more peaceful. The deeper insights which God the Father gives must be paid for with tears. I will send you the book by Seebas [presumably German philosopher and theologian, Christian Ludwig Seebas, 1754–1806], which moved us greatly. May its reading bring you blessing, my child. Only when I know that your faith is firmly rooted in Our Saviour will I be able to die in

peace. Then I will know you to be under faithful protection, wherever you may be. Certainly, we have to wait for the hour in which you will be touched; but I ask one thing of you again and again: do not close your heart, do not think that you have to arm yourself with opposition in order not to give in to me, your mother. Oh, my dear child, it is not a question of me, but only of you.

The letters that Renata quotes from both parents often reproach her for what they see as her bloody-minded resistance to wise counsel. Maria thinks that she must somehow disarm Renata's passive resistance if she is to save her daughter's soul. She succeeded to the extent of prevailing upon Renata to be baptized—an experience the young woman found deeply inauthentic and also morally troubling at a time when she was becoming aware of Nazism and felt that she should be making a stand against it. Of the baptism she writes, "My mother was pleased, while my father had remained at home, offering no comment."

Renata realized early on that their marriage was troubled: "Sometimes I woke in the middle of the night and heard my mother screaming at my father. I heard her throwing heavy objects against the wall and I was frozen with fear that something terrible might happen." And she understood that Albert needed to cede control to Maria in many areas, including parenting, in order to survive in the relationship. Thus could Maria insist on the baptism without apparently considering any feelings the young woman might have, or might wish to explore, about her paternal

Jewish ancestry, and without encountering anything but mute, implied misgivings from her husband. Later she writes that her father "refrained from sharing his inner life and Jewish heritage with me", but quotes a letter in which he says: "it is some kind of satisfaction when you show some interest in Jewish affairs and history."

Renata's portrait of Albert is unwaveringly affectionate and admiring:

> My father was a gentle man. His brown eyes were kind and wise, ready to twinkle at any time. He was not in the habit of telling jokes but could find humor in everyday situations. His specialty was puns, even later in English. His approach to life was philosophical. He spoke deliberately, did not make hasty, superficial judgments. Compassion and sensitivity made him an ideal friend. Unpretentious in appearance and manner, he was perfectly willing to leave center stage to his more flamboyant wife. I was continually amazed at his knowledge of literature, philosophy, classical languages and the arts. It seemed as though his memory had retained all that he had ever learned.

Replace male with female pronouns and many of these sentences could be a description of Renata. Indeed, part of her challenge in life was to establish a woman's identity despite being temperamentally far more like her father than her mother.

Some of the most incisive passages in the autobiography concern the way the young girl, her sentiments now filtered through the language of a sixty-eight-year-old woman, learnt to read her parents' relationship and their very different personalities:

> Birds played a great role in my mother's life, all kinds of birds. As long as I can remember we were surrounded by them. What was it that attracted her to birds? Was it their ability to fly that appealed to her fiercely independent spirit? Yet she always tried to subdue them by force. When a parrot resisted her advances she would grab the bird and pull it out of its cage. The birds would fear her but love my father, who allowed them to approach him on their own.

She tries hard to balance the scales, describing memorable experiences like attending music performances and festivals with Maria, and lights on moments and patterns of less complicated shared time, family weekends spent on a boat outside of Berlin:

> I would explore the area on foot, or go for a swim across the lake and back. Sometimes my mother would join me. She still was a strong swimmer then. Those were some of our best moments together, peacefully swimming side by side, occasionally conversing, feeling thoroughly at home in our favorite element, the water. My father watched us somewhat anxiously from the shore, unable to join us on these excursions. A mild heart condition, dating back to his student days when he was on the rowing team, restricted his physical activities, and he only swam in shallow water.

Albert's anxiousness contrasts here, as in many places in the narrative, with Maria's adventurousness. Renata writes: "I was never able to join the battle lines of the feminists," not because she didn't believe in feminism, but because "I had lived with one of the most emancipated career women imaginable. My mother was a true career woman who set her personal ambition above anything else." This too was a poisoned chalice: Maria provided a template for female autonomy, but her often narcissistic and manipulative parenting made the achievement of adult autonomy a lifelong struggle for her daughter. But Renata was eternally grateful that her mother—not her risk-averse Jewish father—saw the writing on the wall in the 1930s and insisted that the family leave Germany. Late in *Detours and By-ways* she offers this conciliatory assessment of Maria: "Being a mother was not a natural role for her, although she loved me in her own way."

After their marriage, Renata's parents had moved into an apartment in Lichtenberg, which they shared with Maria's best friend, Charlotte Baudot. Lotte, as she was known, was childless after a failed marriage, and became the first and perhaps the most important mentor figure in Renata's life. The young girl referred to her as Tante Lottchen: "I became the child that circumstances had denied her, and she gave me all the love, tenderness and understanding that my mother had not been able to show." The young girl would "bathe" in Lotte's love and approval; they "would take walks together and I would tell her of all the things that occupied my mind or that troubled me. I always felt good about myself when I was with Tante Lottchen."

Four decades later, I had the same feeling in Renata's company. She was a woman "I feel touched in the contemplation of."

Another older friend and confidante was Hertha Hoover, a voice student of Maria's who married Maria's one sibling, her young brother, Karl-Ernst. In their home, too, Renata encountered a disturbed marriage. The vital, fun-loving and optimistic Hertha was quite unlike Karl-Ernst, a physically frail, recessive man who had been profoundly damaged by the family's traumas. Though Hertha was seventeen years older than Renata, the two "confided in each other like teenage girls." One such exchange was to have lasting effects: when Renata was about twenty, Hertha revealed to her that she and Albert were romantically involved. Renata writes:

> My first reaction was: "Why does she tell me this?" I was only too aware of the problems in my parents' marriage and had always wondered at my parents' acquiescence. Extra-marital affairs were common in our society, and this was not a frivolous relationship on either side. They both lived with difficult, egocentric partners and drew comfort and strength from each other. Both my mother and Karl-Ernst remained ignorant to the end of their days, strange as it may seem. Perhaps I could have preferred to remain ignorant myself. Having to keep this knowledge hidden in the back of my mind did not make my position in the family easier in later developments.

The ignorance of Maria and her brother was the more

remarkable when, shortly after the war, Hertha and Karl-Ernst joined Maria and Albert in the house in Newtonville, near Boston. Here, under this one roof, the covert relationship continued until Karl-Ernst's and Maria's deaths.

It was in this house that Mark lived with Hertha, the sole survivor of that complex domestic arrangement, when he came to Brandeis. Sometimes when speaking to Mark by phone from campus, I'd hear a bird shrieking in the background. Maria's last parrot had outlived her.

—∞∞—

In late 1938, Renata's parents learned that their application to immigrate to the US had been provisionally approved. They made their way in high spirits to the US Consulate for their first interview, but:

> we were not prepared for the scenes that confronted us. The waiting rooms were filled with desperate Jews: orthodox, assimilated German Jews, intellectuals and working-class families— all consumed by the same feverish urge to be admitted to the United States ... The Consul and his staff receded into a detached, impersonal attitude to protect themselves against this daily assault upon their emotions.

She goes on: "The realization of being among the lucky ones has not left me all these years. I feel an obligation not to waste my life and to fight prejudice in every form."

She went through weeks of farewells in Berlin "as if in a dream" and, after a storm-tossed voyage from Hamburg, arrived in early March 1939 at Ellis Island. A few days later the family took a train to Boston, where Renata soon found employment as a secretarial assistant in a medical research laboratory.

In Boston, Maria resumed voice teaching, Albert did his American medical training, resumed practice as an ophthalmologist, and in due course Renata became engaged to an organist and family friend, Ludwig Theis. She had been infatuated with a musician in Germany and had drifted briefly into an engagement with another man before the war. When Ludwig proposed marriage, just six months after the family's arrival in the US, Renata accepted—"Was there any strong reason not to marry him?" They had a congenial friendship based around music and those in their circle seemed to assume that they would become man and wife. A more worldly woman in her early twenties might have discerned one reason at least for caution when her fiancé resisted all sexual intimacy during courtship, arguing that they should abstain until after the wedding. But Renata was drifting: "Like so many times in my life, I failed to take control of my future but did what was expected of me." The wedding passed like an enfevered dream:

> The elaborate ceremony and dinner that followed affected me like a stage play. Was this actually my wedding, or was I performing a role in a play? The script had been written by others, and the scenery was strange to me. All I had to do was speak my lines and act the part of a bride. I was slightly feverish from a throat infection and attributed my disturbing feelings of dissociation to this physical cause.

The marriage was never consummated and eventually Ludwig admitted that "a lifelong masochistic tendency" had made him impotent in any "normal relationship." Masturbation, and orgasms during some of his emotional organ improvisations, provided his outlet. He had hoped that marriage would "bring a change." Renata, who had learnt not to expect too much of marriage, was prepared to drift on in a union that was otherwise congenial, especially as she was finding fulfillment in her developing career as a singer in Boston. A young American composer, "E," conducted a chamber orchestra in which she performed and soon became her accompanist in recitals of songs he had composed.

One day, after a rehearsal in her apartment, their conversation turned to more personal things:

> He had been aware that something was not right in my life, and for the first time I let go of my reserve and talked openly about my marriage. E released repressions and inhibitions that had built up in me over years. I was swept along on a powerful wave of new sensations and responses that carried me out of my self-imposed prison. The change in me was immediate and profound. Blinders fell off my eyes and I saw my life in a different light. After this afternoon I knew that a return to my former ways was impossible.

On a trip to New York to prepare for upcoming musical engagements she found the space, away from husband and mother, for further reflection: "I looked at myself more realistically, saw my diffidence, my weak acceptance of a frustrating situation that already had lasted too long. What was I waiting for?" She returned to Boston and told a shattered Ludwig that she was leaving him. "It was difficult to listen to his pleas and his confessions of guilt," but "I closed my ears and started divorce proceedings." Her parents, who had known about her difficulties, supported her decision. But her mother's reaction convinced Renata that she needed to get away not just from Ludwig but from Maria as well: "Thank God," Maria said when Renata announced the separation, "now you will be completely mine again."

Renata packed her bags and moved a four-hour drive away to New York.

She found a large room in an apartment on Eighty-Third Street near West End Avenue, which she shared with two other young women and the apartment's owner, Linda, who claimed to work on Wall Street. Gaudily dressed and made-up, Linda's efforts to disguise her age were wholly unavailing, but she proved to be a woman of many parts:

> Linda had it all worked out: on Monday and Thursday nights she'd entertain old Peter, a pot-bellied, bald, good-natured fellow in his seventies. He paid Linda's bills. On Wednesdays she received a mysterious, dark-haired young man whom we never got to meet. He quietly slipped in and out of the apartment. In his case we were not sure who was paying whom.

Rather typically, Renata describes her own private life at the time as a self-estranged state of liberation. After her encounter with E, "I found myself unable to harness this sexual drive. I looked for nothing but to satisfy a physical need, shying away from another emotional involvement."

Working in a clerical job while taking on musical engagements, she settled into an uncomplicated relationship with a young German chemist by the name of Erik. Since neither of them wanted a binding commitment she had no hesitation in responding to an advertisement and auditioning for a touring opera company under the management of an impresario named Bill Reuterman, "a master of the art of evasion and double talk." At a rehearsal she met a man who "looked the part of the Italian singer: strong and barrel-chested, with an abundance of dark, wavy hair, brown eyes and an aquiline nose. He was agile and seemed to be all over the place." This was Joe, and it soon became obvious that he "took an interest in me." The feeling however was by no means mutual. On the day of the tour's departure, "I staged a tender, emotional farewell with Erik right in front of the bus, making sure that Joe would watch it." Undaunted, Joe was elaborately solicitous toward the unattached young woman during the tour, helping with her heavy case, attending to her every need.

Occasionally Renata would sing the part of Stefano in Donizetti's opera "Don Gregorio," a role that included a fencing scene with Gregorio. Since Joe was playing Gregorio and Renata knew nothing of fencing he suggested that she come to his room for lessons. She declined this invitation: "I had a pretty good idea of the kind of 'fencing' he had in mind and made sure that the instruction took place backstage instead."

As the tour continued on its westward and increasingly impecunious journey, Joe's persistence started to pay dividends. After a performance at the University in Madison, Wisconsin, he prevailed on her to take a walk along a nearby lake:

> By now I had observed Joe in many situations and had begun to appreciate the qualities that made him stand out among the other singers. There was a solid core to his personality, he was sincere and showed concern for others. As we walked along the lake on this clear autumn night I realized that the attraction was now mutual. I did not yet realize that it was going to be Joe who would give my life stability and direction, and whose uncritical emotional support would finally allow me to develop into a more secure human being.

This development and so much that followed now received a helping hand from the rogue impresario Reuterman. In Omaha, Nebraska, seven weeks into what was to have been a seven-month program, he announced that the tour was out of cash, leaving those who hadn't already left after seeing the writing on the wall stranded. The tour bus drivers, having to return to New York anyway, provided a free ride home. Renata, having fifty dollars left in travelers checks, was able to buy some food for what remained of the troupe. On arrival Joe and Renata took a hotel room near Times

Square to recover and ponder their options.

Renata soon rented a room of her own, took a clerical job and continued to seek musical engagements. Four decades later she wondered why she did not then take more decisive steps to establish a secure life: "Obviously I was not ready for further drastic changes. The pattern of passive acceptance had not been broken entirely. I still needed more self-confidence." The relationship with Joe continued to develop. A visit to introduce him to her parents in Boston seems to have gone well and Renata writes with warm amusement, sometimes qualified by distaste at the formulaic ostentation of weddings, funerals and other rituals, about the Italian-American world she encountered at the Maimone home. She came to love and admire Joe's mother, Nancy Nunziata, for her sincerity, warmth, freedom from prejudice, and good sense. This woman from a peasant background, far less sophisticated than her prospective daughter-in-law, welcomed Renata warmly into her family and provided the young woman with a viable model of family life.

For her part, Nancy was not surprised when Joe married a foreign woman. After leaving school during the Depression he worked in a supermarket whose clientele included Mme Textrude, a Norwegian soprano from the Metropolitan Opera Company. When Mme Textrude learnt of his musical interests and talent she invited him to move into her home where she gave him voice lessons and introduced him to a world of musicians and artists which captured his imagination. In 1996 Renata wrote in a letter to me:

"Joe fell in love with what I represent, rather than who I am." Being Renata, she wasn't about to romanticize the backstory or to pretend that the resultant union between these very different people was perfectly fulfilling: "We had to learn to compromise between my German spirit of independence and his Sicilian expectations of a woman's role." As she wrote in another letter: "Ideal relationships only exist in fairy tales."

Their makeshift lifestyle of part-time musical engagements and part-time work came to an abrupt halt when, in early 1949, Renata found she was pregnant. They married on 24 March 1949 and Joe took a full-time job in the insurance industry, becoming a much-loved salesman renowned for singing and telling gags to his clients. Without consulting her husband, Renata organized a loan from Albert, with which they purchased their first home in Glen Head, New York.

When Jeff arrived in October, Renata's life reached perhaps its greatest turning point:

> For the first time in my life I was not working toward some artistic goals, or working at a job outside the home. Suddenly I was thrown into the role of mother and housewife. I wonder how I would have felt had I been established in a profession … It had been a totally self-centered existence. Now I was responsible for a new life, had definite tasks and duties which I did not wish to relegate to someone else. Two

things were clear to me: first, I wanted to have a warm, close relationship with any children of mine. They should not have to turn to someone else for affection and understanding. Second, I did not want to think of children as my property to mould in my image. They should be able to follow their own inclinations without fear of not being able to fulfill any expectations I might have of them.

In his eulogy, Mark, who was born in January 1952, described Renata as "a patient, supporting but quietly ambitious mother" who "insisted on music" as a central aspect of family life. Mark became a fine professional cellist, who continues to play semi-professionally to this day despite retraining as an environmental engineer. His implication—that Renata was a more ambitious parent than she apparently wished to be—would not have surprised her; she knew that no one can ever wholly discard their own conditioning.

While her own family life provided happy years that Renata had never known before, her parents' situation remained intensely distressing. Hertha and Karl-Ernst had moved in with them in the Newtonville house after horrendous personal tragedies in Germany: Hertha had been raped by Russian soldiers, their house burnt down, and their only child, Klaus, with whom Hertha had a sustaining relationship, drowned while swimming at the age of eighteen. Renata's frequent trips to Boston to visit the foursome were a source of constant anguish and confusion:

It is still very difficult for me to analyse the

conflicting feelings that tore at me every time I entered the house in Newtonville. I was fully aware of everything that went on, saw how each of them lived in his or her own private hell, and I felt utterly helpless.

She was certain her mother never had an inkling of Hertha and Albert's relationship because Marie "was far too sure of her power over my father." She had no reason to think that Karl-Ernst ever suspected anything. She adds: "To this day it is a mystery how four people can live under one roof for so many years and know so little about each other."

Fearing that the tensions in the house might exacerbate her mother's condition, Renata tried to persuade Hertha to find another home for her and Karl-Ernst. Both Hertha and Albert refused to countenance this suggestion, and as Maria's mental health worsened Hertha's presence became more necessary than ever, as a source of emotional support for Albert and as a carer for Maria. Maria, by contrast, avoided sick people at all costs and "never once went upstairs to see Karl-Ernst" when he became terminally ill. He died in about 1964. It is one of the most haunting ironies of this painful history that when Maria became too confused and unwell to be cared for at home as the 1960s wore on, it was Hertha who visited her every day in her special care facility because Albert's heart condition restricted the frequency of his visits, and that Hertha became the center of Maria's world: "My mother was now like a child in her hands, she trusted Hertha and no one else."

It is impossible to capture the full complexity of what

occurred when the life-histories of Maria Elsberg and Hertha Hoover converged: it would seem that Hertha, who lived on until 1990, long after the other three had died, saved her sister-in-law's marriage by conducting a thirty-year affair with Maria's husband. If this affair may not exactly have saved Hertha's marriage, it seems to have made life tolerable for a woman who was married to a profoundly depressed man, had lost her only child and suffered an atrocity during the war.

However much pain all of this caused Renata, it gave her rare insight into the labyrinthine recesses of human need and an equally rare tolerance for the moral compromises and adaptations that decent people can find necessary for psychic survival.

The letters that the now intermittently confused and paranoid Maria wrote to Renata from hospital and special care are distressing to read:

> My dearest: writing is no longer an easy job, for I do not <u>really</u> live and can only repeat what the radio tells me. My contact with my <u>former</u> home is a very loose one; I get the things that I cannot get here or Hertha reads an article to me. She has made up her mind that I shall never return to your father, so complete of her mind—must try to adapt myself to it without hating them. That is not easy. Therefore if you could manage a visit when the weather gets better, I would very welcome … answer this question <u>why</u> do I grow so old? Is it a punishment?

In an extraordinary letter to his daughter, written I think some time in the early 1960s, Albert touches on his wife's propensity for hatred. It would seem that this letter was occasioned by Renata's distress about Maria's attitude to her:

> You look for an explanation of Muttchen's present negative attitude in the wrong place, and you have thereby offended Hertha, which surely was not your intention. Why should it? What interest would Hertha have in putting a wedge between you and your mother? The opposite is true. Hertha has always tried to put things right, because Muttchen's dislike of you dates back a long way and flares up time and again. She has often complained about your uncommunicativeness, and not without reason, that you never spontaneously talk about yourself, that one has to drag everything out of you. I suppose this is a kind of uneasiness toward your parents, and also toward Hertha.

He continues:

> It is unfortunately true that her [Maria's] nature has always been closer to hatred than to love. There never has been a happy medium, only exaggerated love or hatred. That had already started with her attitude toward my family. And later on you have witnessed it with our friends and acquaintances, with her students, and especially with Hertha and her brother Karl-Ernst. This, her nature, has become more and more pronounced. And at

present you are the victim. You must also consider the oppressive heritage in Muttchen's family. The pathological character traits were always present, overshadowed by high intelligence. Also for me it had been difficult and took a long time until I finally recognized it.

Since Albert's English seems to have been very good, it is unlikely that he would have used the term "dislike" to characterize Maria's attitude to Renata loosely. This must have been devastating for her to read, however much she feared, suspected, or knew it to be the case. Little wonder that Renata writes of her family, that despite her best efforts, "it was impossible for me to find a comfortable place within this triangle."

An earlier letter from Albert, dated 1959, is a moving instance of a fine man trying to negotiate the fateful moral complexities of his own life and to explain them to his adult child, who was then forty-two. His tone toward her is deeply appreciative and it must have been a relief to be able to explain to his daughter that his marital vow to her mother had, in Shakespeare's words, been "more honour'd in the breach than the observance."

I thank you very much for your personal letter which showed me your understanding of all the problems involving Muttchen's mental state. In spite of all her faults—increasing in stature with age—I lived with her for more than forty-five years. I loved her and still we are bound together, even when love changed to the utmost pity for her. We had our ups and downs and all in all she was a companion more than worthwhile living with. I needed her energy and willpower [to leave Germany] and will always be thankful to her and willing to forget everything else.

In July 1967 Albert suffered a massive heart attack in Newtonville and was on life-support when Renata arrived from New York. On her second day there, her father, after making only eye contact, managed to scrawl these words with a pencil: "Turn the machine off." And, "What did Muttchen say?" He died that night, aged seventy-eight.

The day after his death a shaken Renata visited Maria in her care facility and told her as sensitively as she could: "Today I am bringing very sad news, Dad died last night." This section of the autobiography closes thus:

She looked at me without any change of expression and asked her customary first question: "Did you bring me chocolate?" I suppose I should have been grateful that she no longer felt any emotion, but I realized how far removed she was from reality.

―――

Maria died six months later, in January 1968, aged eighty-three, the huge turbulent life-force that had sustained her now having taken strange leave of her body: "I watched her hands make aimless, fluttering motions on the covers, as though they were directed by an outside force." Writing fifteen years later of her mother, Renata "cannot judge how many of her traits were based upon her personality, and how many were manifestations of her chronic manic-depressive cycles"; but she writes of her as "a tragic figure" rather than a malevolent one—a typically magnanimous assessment given that Renata's "love for her was always clouded by her constant attempts to hurt me in my most sensitive areas, and by alternatively exaggerating my achievements and destroying my fragile self-esteem."

—◦◦◦—

Renata would first have heard from Mark about me less than two years after she had buried her mother. A different person might have cautioned her son against drawing too close to an acquaintance prone to depression or shied away from engagement with yet another melancholic soul. After all, as Holden Caulfield laconically observes, "you don't have to be a bad guy to depress somebody."

Looking back, I'm astonished at her willingness to welcome me into her life so soon and after all she'd been through, and by her capacity to do so with such uncomplicated warmth. An apocalyptically discommodious couch – "too short for stretching out and the cover too narrow for curling up"—is threatened in the Tanakh if the Jews don't mend their ways. Renata's sofa in the living room was in contrast a commodious and consoling thing, and became the scene of many long conversations. It had alternating vertical ochre, mustard, white and black stripes, the fabric heavily textured and slightly abrasive through a thin shirt. Otherwise it was remarkably comfortable: long enough to lie flat without having to elevate feet or head on one of its arms, restful but firm for sitting up, its middle cushion a convenient resting place for books, writing drafts and other appurtenance of good talk.

After retirement Joe spent much of his time at his golf club so that if Mark and I arrived from Waltham in the early afternoon, a typical, smiling, hyperbolic greeting from Renata would be: "Esteemed Dr. Freudman, it is an honor again to be able to entertain you in your family home. Sir Joseph is holding court at the golf club. Can I offer you some refreshment to assist in your recovery from your arduous journey?" Refreshment provided, the talk would commence, sometimes with Mark, sometimes just Renata and me as he adjourned to the music room for cello practice.

She would often start serious talks with: "So, how has it been these last few weeks?" My habitual need for approval usually inclined me to begin with good and successful news—say an "A" on an essay, or encouraging words from a professor. She had a way of saying "*veerry good*" that put enthusiastic, but not quite effusive, emphasis on both words. And then she would nod, her smiling eyes inviting elaboration, which I would gladly provide. If I was feeling robust, talk would turn to other things. On one occasion, having read about American "crooners," I asked her how someone like Sinatra would compare technically with a high quality trained opera singer.

"No comparison," she said firmly. "There is no need for proper voice production with a microphone. Sinatra can convey feeling and he knows his audience. He sings about very American fantasies and disappointments. But a good opera singer has much more control, modulation, artistry.

Sinatra's voice is a blunt instrument. It has a big turning circle like a Buick. An opera singer is a different beast."

If I was feeling burdened, however, I would soon get round to my current worries, no matter how much I had resolved not to. I often told her, for instance, about the most impressive and charismatic of my teachers, Professor Allen Grossman. Though he was kind and encouraging to me, I was, I told her, so intimidated by his erudition and fierce intellectual focus that I felt overwhelmed in his presence and, perversely, becalmed by my most compelling source of inspiration. And already my slow reading, migraines and poor memory were imposing their limits upon what my limitless ambition bade me to do.

Renata said: "It is early days. If you want to be good at something you're going to model yourself on people who are already good at it, and that can be intimidating. But that comes with the turf and the best thing is not to worry about the end-point, about how good you can be. Enjoy the challenge. Who knows what a man as finely organized as you might achieve? Some of the musicians who visited our family apartment [in Berlin] were so inspiring that I fell in love with music; but when my mother's voice lessons started I couldn't enjoy it. All I was left with was ambition."

I was struck at the time by the slightly antiquated ring of "finely organized" but gathered that in using the term Renata was in effect ushering me into esteemed interwar European cultural company. As I've tried to negotiate my highly strung (a modern approximation to "finely organized") personality and its various complexities and inner resistances over the years, Renata's apt and encouraging phrase has stayed with me.

Since I was not infrequently recumbent and becalmed by worry on that couch of compassion, it became a family joke that Maria and Albert had snatched it from Freud's study in Vienna and brought it to the New World in the same consignment as the Steinway. Years later, when Renata and Joe moved to one of Renata's favorite coastal towns— Bayville, Long Island—the Steinway went to Mark and his wife Margaretha and the sofa took up residence in the new home. It was there for me, welcoming as ever, when I made occasional visits to the United States.

Often Renata and I sat at either end of the sofa, chatting over tea and health foods. Renata was a superb listener. There are people whose attentive listening can arouse unease: they tilt their head slightly sideways, sizing you up unsmilingly with one eye. Renata always made direct face-on eye contact, those kindly eyes seeming seldom to blink, yet also not to stare. Her look seemed to acknowledge who you were, or wished to be. It gave you space to speak, to think aloud, if you would, but seemed to lay no requirements upon you. That special receptiveness often seemed akin to a smile, as if talk between friends, no matter how serious or troubled, was a pleasure.

She herself spoke with considered directness, as though much had been deeply pondered; yet it was offered up spontaneously, as the occasion allowed, without artifice or strategic intent. There was a stillness about her: she didn't gesticulate much and seemed able to sit comfortably, back straight and seldom shifting, for long periods. She was deeply reflective and deeply sincere. Nothing seemed to be off-limits, but nor was there any awkwardness if either of us, for whatever reason, didn't want to go where a conversation was heading.

Only once was there a misunderstanding. On one occasion, having thought her unwelcoming, I'd left early, communicating my displeasure to Mark. When I got back to Brandeis there was a phone message from my mother saying that an upset Renata had phoned her in Australia to try to set things straight with me. It was easily done: Renata had quite reasonably been preoccupied during my visit and, typically, I'd taken it as a personal affront.

What drew us together? Michel de Montaigne, explaining his love for a male friend, puts it with disarming simplicity: "because it was he, because it was I." Any friend of either of her beloved sons would have been a friend of Renata's. But though this began our friendship, it wasn't what sustained it. Perhaps my being Jewish, literary and not involved in the world of music echoed positive aspects of Renata's relationship with her father. Like her, I was haunted by the Holocaust and often questioned her about it, and I also had a close acquaintance with the destructive power of depression. Yet far from activating Renata's long-honed self-protective impulses, my depressive tendencies seemed to arouse in her a depth of empathic concern that is characteristic of deep friendships.

Between reflective friends, friendship itself becomes a subject of reflection, and though we didn't talk a lot about why we had so much to say and to share across generations and continents, our conversations were edged with a kind of urgency. We were both deeply committed to and interested in the quality of friendships we had with others. Profound friendship has at its heart an opaque radiance that resists exhaustive explanation. I write about my mentor-friendship with Renata and aspects of her life as a woman in a spirit of inquiring fondness and appreciation, comfortable in the knowledge that, not least because I am a man writing a woman's life, there is much that I cannot and do not need to know.

Friendship can issue from many sources, one of them being the disposition in one or both parties to befriend. This disposition ran deep in Renata, who made close friends throughout her life; it also ran deep in me. Her self-protective diffidence, a response to her mother and the complexities in her parents' marriage, seems not to have applied to friends, especially from the time Renata unburdened herself to "E."

She had experienced a warm and successful mentor-friendship with an older person in Lotte, and I had experienced such a relationship with my maternal grandfather, Roy Isles. We brought to our friendship fond recollections of these earlier bonds and certain interpersonal skills that we had learned through them. One such skill was honesty, and as a mentor-friend she could be quite firm in dismissing my self-indulgent excesses.

Once, when we'd been talking about her mother and I was feeling low, I suggested to Renata that I might have bipolar disease. She wasn't having a bar of that; indeed her reply was uncharacteristically sharp and dismissive.

"Oh, nonsense! That is ridiculous! Of course not!"

She saw me, as she could see herself looking back, as a young person with a lot of promise, a bumpy road to travel and a good life in prospect, given increased self-confidence, maturity and some guidance. This perception of my difficulties was itself very generous, compared to what she'd been through my troubles were a graze in a rose garden.

Friendship also involves work—the work required to maintain the bond, to deepen each party's understanding of their life and their world. This work needs a shared belief in friendship itself; often, as between Renata and myself, a belief that friendship is an indispensable component of flourishing, of the Good Life. Friendship can take many forms—common causes and commitments to action, for instance, or narratives of self-disclosure within a constantly evolving shared sense of value. Friends can judge and criticize one another, but solicitous regard rather than cool appraisal is, I think, the métier of true friendship.

Friendship also seems to welcome, even need, genres. It often matters whether we deem someone a close or more distant friend, a lover, a soul mate. Such distinctions of course are approximate and fluid; they can shift over time, and some relationships seem to defy categorization. But uncertainty in such matters can be a source of genuine unease: "Can I trust this person as I would a close friend?" Uncertainty can be thrilling, as in the *frisson* of not quite knowing whether a friendship is subliminally sexual or not.

Certainty, on the other hand, can bring ease and security: to say "this is a friendship not a romantic relationship" can be freeing, allowing friendship to be what it is. Knowing what genre you are in can involve discussion, even disputation: "I want more than a friendship!" But not necessarily. Some relationships seem to settle readily into a genre, a rhythm, a pattern, without needing to be managed or redefined. Both parties work at the relationship—at making it work and allowing it to grow—but with an agreed and relatively untroubled sense of what it is they are working on.

That's how it was with Renata. The reader could be forgiven for interpreting the present chapter as the narrative of a surrogate son, but such a reading largely misses the point. Renata and I were nothing like that close. In later years we could go for six or nine months without corresponding, and when her life was ebbing peacefully away over many hours her concern was only for her family. She did not ask for a message to be sent to me, and nor would I have expected her to. I was important to her, as were her other close friends, and indeed other younger people whom she had befriended and helped; but friendship was one thing, family another. Renata, who had been compelled from an early age to contend with so much psychic disorder around her, was very good at sustaining subtle emotional distinctions: between her two families—Elsberg and Maimone – and between various forms of human connection: family, friends, and valued acquaintances.

Keeping the two families mentally separate while remaining committed to each in its way must have been an enormous strain on her inner reserves. But as she explains, it was a matter of both choice and necessity:

> At home I rarely spoke about my visits to Newtonville. Joe's straightforward nature would have found it difficult to understand the currents and cross-currents that governed relationships in my parents' home. I did not want anything to interfere with the peace and harmony in my own family. Nothing would have been gained by drawing them into these struggles. My own family life and Newtonville—I kept these two spheres apart by a conscious effort.

In this effort she was assisted by a skill akin to her habit of passive resistance: compartmentalization—the psychic mechanism that can cordon one domain of experience off from another, or from various other aspects of psychic life. In its pathological forms—a concentration camp guard who could commit atrocities during the day and delight in Goethe by the fire in the evening—compartmentalization can be terrifying. But in its more benign forms it is an essential skill for psychic survival that we all practice to some degree. Renata's earlier feelings of dissociation, passivity, emotional vacancy—responses that incensed her mother—were probably unwitting forms of compartmentalization. *Detours and By-ways* shows her practicing this skill more discerningly as she grows, and becoming aware that it has both positive and negative implications: it permits her room to grow and allows her to keep the Newtonville and Long Island families relatively separate; it could seem like insurmountable reserve to those close to her.

When I mentioned Renata's first marriage to Mark he was surprised to hear that she had been married before. She could share that signal piece of information with me more readily because as an outsider I was exempt from the compartmentalizing that helped her build a much happier family life than the one she had grown up in.

My parents were also both very good at friendship and, like Renata, my mother Fleur had emerged from a disturbing childhood determined to provide parenting and a home that was very different from her experience. Like Renata, too, she had a very difficult relationship with a powerful maternal figure. What Fleur didn't do so well—at least not to my satisfaction—was boundaries.

A more ebullient and mercurial person than Renata, Fleur responded to her past by seeking to tear down the curtains and let the light of psychological understanding flood in. The Renata who unburdened herself to "E," to other friends and in her autobiography, needed emotional release and understanding too, but she also needed to compartmentalize. In me she found a young person, interested and often expert in the complexities of the inner world, with whom she could debrief about Newtonville while on the sofa in Roslyn Harbor, without imperiling the stability of the family life she and Joe had created. With Renata I could relax into a habit of psychological exploration that Fleur had done so much to foster in and for me, but without the son's concern that boundaries might not adequately be respected. Just occasionally Renata too would push boundaries, generally when anxiety about her own family inclined her to confide in me about Mark, Jeff or her marriage in ways that made me uncomfortable. But being good at boundaries she would quickly draw back when she sensed my unease.

Though this is not the narrative of a surrogate son, it is in some respects, then, a biographical portrait of a surrogate mother. Renata's particular blend of reserve and openness would have been appealing to me at any time, and being relatively young, troubled and a long way from home, she did in some ways fill the role of mother for me in my twenties, and beyond. Fleur felt like a strange fusion of mother and troubled younger sister. With Renata I felt on firmer ground.

———

It was mid-winter, fifteen months into our friendship, when we set out from Brandeis for New York. The campus was feet-deep in snow, car wheels secure only where great tracts of salt had melted the ice. On a good day it was over four hours from Waltham to Roslyn Harbor. This was going to be a very long drive.

Half an hour in, the old Saab started to complain. Heating became too much of an effort. We pulled in at a gas station and got from the trunk the ugly green anoraks that Renata had helped us buy some months before. (I still have mine.) These kept the upper body warm but our legs shivered in drafts from unseen gaps and crevices. Presently the gray sky released cascading snow, lovely to behold, except that it accumulated on the windscreen so fast that you had to look out of a side window to see the full majesty of the storm. The old windscreen wipers struggled manfully for a while, moaning as they nudged the white deposits aside, sighed to a pause, and our whole world turned white. If there was a gas station in the vicinity it was not visible, and, unable to see anything but the side of the highway, we pulled over. You could not drive in this without wipers and Mark thought the storm could last for hours.

The best bet seemed to be to operate the wipers manually from within the car with string. So Mark fetched some rough cord from the boot, attached ends to each wiper, fed the ends in through the small triangular side windows, and I took up the reins in wet woolen gloves. Remarkably, this worked well enough to resume our journey, though shards of frigid air from the windows' open slits cut so hard into our temples and sinuses that we had to pull our hoods right up, zipping them to just below our noses. We peered intently through the fur-lined apertures at the road. The one carrying us from prestigious campus to middle-class suburban home was the very road Kerouac wished not to travel. Nor, as it turned out, did the Saab. Soon, noises that Mark did not recognize started to reverberate through the cabin: clunks, grindings, rattles, squeaks—sounds more befitting the prairie than the highway. This did not bode well but what were we to do? We wiped, bumped and rattled on until the life force started to ebb from the elderly vehicle. Dashboard dials said we were losing power;

the accelerator flapped untethered like a limp flipper. We ground to a halt.

The world we stepped out into was white but far from wondrous. The cold water in my gloves froze; there was nothing in sight. Mobile phones were a thing of the future. We needed assistance to get to some place from which we could summon help. Eventually a passing van pulled over, the driver offering to take us to the next turnpike, a few miles up ahead. There a kindly man in a tollbooth the size of a shower cubicle let Mark ring home and SOS Jeff who, as it happened, was working as a mechanic in a Saab dealership on Long Island at the time.

"You goddamn university types!" he huffed amusedly, then set out to rescue us.

Three hours later he arrived; the shivering no-hopers hopped into the heated bliss of his late model sedan, and off we went to inspect the old vehicle. After running a few perfunctory tests Jeff delivered his assessment: "Goodnight nurse! Dead as a dodo! Bro, your car is fucked. Say goodbye to it. We're outa here!"

"But can you leave a car beside the road like that?" I asked, this not being a familiar practice in the Antipodes.

"Don't worry," said Jeff, "there are guys cruising round in vans who can dismantle your car and drive off with it in pieces in the time it takes you to pee beside the road. They'll be all over it like ants on a corpse. Tomorrow there'll be nothing left but bones."

And so, about eight hours after leaving Waltham, we pulled into the family driveway with Jeff and staggered into the living room looking like famished castaways.

"*Oh my God!*" exclaimed Renata. "What *happened?!*"

As we explained, this normally composed soul dissolved into paroxysms of laugher. She laughed so hard she had to sit down for fear of falling. She heaved to catch her breath. She took off her glasses and wiped her eyes.

"Australian-run manual windscreen wipers!" she spluttered, and broke up again.

"Are they back yet?" boomed a voice from across the corridor.

"Oh yeah, the spring chickens are back," replied Jeff.

"So you got that goddamned thing going again, ha?" said Joe as he joined us in the living room.

"Well, no," Mark replied, a touch sheepishly. "It had reached its use-by date. It would have to have been towed all the way back to Long Island and that would have cost more than it was worth."

"Yup," said Jeff. "That car is one dead duck!"

"Goddamnit!" fumed Joe. "You left a perfectly good car beside the road?"

"Perfectly good except that it can never be driven again," Jeff jovially interposed.

Incensed, Joe continued to query the wisdom of our decision, our sanity, the moral wherewithal of university students, and much else.

Occasionally I'd glance at the still-seated Renata, her eyes full of laughter that her throat dared not release. Eventually she stood up and said something like: "Joe, it was a very old car. It probably wasn't safe for Mark to drive

235

for much longer anyway. You bought it secondhand ten years ago. It's served us well. Jeff would have got it home if he could. The boys are home safely. That's the main thing. Half your golf buddies sell cars and you sell insurance to car salesmen. Why not get on the phone and find Mark a new car?"

"God-damn-it!" huffed Joe, blundering back to his den and picking up the phone.

———

In classic and wonderfully rich discussions of friendship, Aristotle identifies three main types: friendship based on utility, friendship based on pleasure, and perfect friendship based on goodness. He suggests that the third kind subsumes the first two, since two absolutely good people connected by friendship will be useful to one another (utility) in providing perfect, reciprocal friendship; a source of pleasure to one another, given that to a profoundly good person friendship based on goodness is a source of sublime pleasure; and good, because both parties, being good, love and support one another and delight in seeing one another flourish. Some philosophers have argued that this picture of friendship is logically untenable because, for instance, utility and absolute regard for the other person are conflicting ideas.

My friendship with Renata suggests other possibilities. I wouldn't say that we were both deeply good: I'd say that she was and I wasn't. I don't mean that I was a louse, but I was less mature, more selfish and strategic, more inclined to cut moral corners than she. But this moral asymmetry didn't seem to matter; in fact from my point of view it was for the best, because in a mentor-like relationship one hopefully learns from the mentor not just to be better at *something*, but to be better, *period*.

I was also fortunate that Renata, a refugee from the sort of grandiose and unstable aspirational self-imaginings of youth to which I was prone, provided an example of firm, undeceived, realistic self-appraisal. When sciatica had laid Joe low in late 1997 and his Sicilian expectations of the woman's role in the household were straining Renata's patience, she wrote to me: "I am poor material for sainthood." This was more than an aside. Her survivor's conscience set high standards and she was not one to let herself off the moral hook. Yet she had a particular gift and inclination for mirroring one's own self in a way that put one on better terms with one's self, as when she writes in a letter of our sometimes parallel exercise regimes in Bayville, she in the water, me on land: "Whenever I have been doing my daily swim to Piping Rock (including yesterday), I see the phantom of the Australian professor, floppy hat, flailing arms, determined stride, passing me on the shore and waving to the solitary swimmer."

The conversations on that sofa ranged far wider than narrowly personal concerns. We would speak about social and political issues; in rereading her letters of the 1980s and 1990s I'm reminded of her political prescience and insight: she predicted that the then disgraced Newt Gingrich would rise again, that Rupert Murdoch would eventually reap the whirlwind, and noted in August 1996 that "our obsession to impose our style of democracy on other countries (with frequently disastrous results) is a form of colonialism." She wrote in 1997 that my children's generation "will have to choose between adhering to a slowly weakening" social and political system "and the challenge to shape something out of a kaleidoscope of converging foreign cultures." She hated any form of prejudice and was pessimistic about the longer-term future, notwithstanding her own constructive attitude to life: "Our two countries share in the abominable treatment of the native population and in the firm conviction that the 'white' race is a priori superior to all other races and cultures. Thank God, we won't live to see the demise of Western culture, but it seems inevitable." This apocalyptic tone was quite typical—"The world is absurd, nature will have the last word"—and she saw the complexities of personal agency with which she struggled within a larger metaphysical context that was preeminently governed by chance: a professed "non-believer" she wrote in August 1992: "Chance rules our lives, from the moment of conception."

This sweeping formulation, which comes in a letter in which she agonizes over the "frightful injustice we see all around us," somewhat simplifies the position that informs *Detours and By-ways* and much of what she said and wrote to me. The autobiography, after all, is about struggling through to a form of selfhood that can "take control and make deliberate choices." Chance will determine the general context within which we find ourselves and will set some limits to how we can respond to that context; but within those parameters we have the capacity, and indeed the responsibility, to exercise control and make the best choices we can, keeping the needs and rights of others uppermost in our minds. As Renata wrote: "We can't do much more than try to keep our lives as straight as possible and do minimum damage to those around us; in the best case we can hope to exert positive influence given the opportunity."

—⁂—

From the outset our conversations focused a good deal on writing. Renata's past was waiting to be told; the crack was widening. As she recounted bits of her difficult history to me, we also talked about autobiographical writing. I commented on some of her early, shorter pieces; later I read through parts, and then a full draft of *Detours and By-ways*, offering detailed editorial suggestions. It was typical of Renata that she took creative writing classes in order to learn the craft and that she became, as she put in it a short piece entitled "Confessions of a Neophyte Writer," "addicted to the act of writing."

On one occasion I arrived at the Bayville house fatigued after the long flight and woozy with one of my reading migraines that had come on in an archive at Columbia University. In recent letters I'd been explaining to Renata that I was beginning to look more closely at philosophical and psychological theories of the will—of how and to what extent we "make" decisions, and of so-called "pathologies of the will": states in which the will seems paralyzed or enslaved by obsessional or delusional perceptions. It had been agreed in advance that I would edit some of the most recent chunks of *Detours and By-ways* during my visit, but I could only stay for two days before taking a train to Boston.

Seeing how tired I was, Renata immediately led me to the sofa, whereupon I stretched out in familiar fashion while she brewed a cup of coffee. After further polite inquires about my condition she got down to the business at hand: "So, Dr. Freudman, what can you tell your mature-aged student about the will? Please answer in words of one syllable, because I am becoming more mature-aged every day."

Having already read Renata's account of her youthful drifting will in early draft chapters of her autobiography, I angled my rather stumbling summation toward that particular theme, explaining that so-called "weakness of will" had been an important though perplexing philosophical topic since antiquity and that the sort of weakness she wrote about could perhaps be seen under this general heading. When I used a phrase that sometimes bobs up in such discussion—"rationality being dragged about by passion" – she leant forward in her armchair, plying me with further questions. The notion that philosophy and psychology had very specific ways of talking about irrationality, inertia, and other afflictions of the will in a basically "rational" person like her hit a chord. I told Renata that a good place to start was Aristotle's *Nicomachean Ethics*. She had a copy in her study at the end of the corridor, which opened out onto a little balcony overlooking meadows. I stretched out for a doze while she strode determinedly off to start reading.

"This is *fascinating*!" she said when I awoke. "I must nurse my editor back to health so that he can provide further expert advice!"

And so, with the utmost resourcefulness, she conjured ways of keeping me going over the next two days, her solicitude, though genuine, also unabashedly strategic: "What if I give you the next chapter when you've had a rest, and then we take a walk along the beach to clear your head?" …

"What about after the family meal you go to bed early so that you'll have better concentration in the morning?" …

"Maybe I'll just give you a few pages at a time and you can take breaks between each little bunch?" …

I got through all the recent draft material before I left.

Along with that enormous drive to write, Renata had the perfectionist's need to do something extremely well, and was troubled by a fear of failure, of not writing well enough to please discerning readers. When she posted me the manuscript of *Detours and By-ways* in June 1985 the accompanying note said: "Dick, please take off the velvet gloves and don't spare the strict criticism." In a letter of March 1997 she wrote: "I did not do a good job when I attempted my memoirs, I was too concerned about who might read it and avoided digging too deeply into dark corners." How wrong she was!

The covering letter that came with the manuscript in June 1985 said that writing her past "has served its original purpose, being a document for children, grandchildren and some interested friends, besides having a therapeutic effect on its author." Her reservations about finding a wider audience concerned what she perceived to be its esthetic limitations: "It has shown me what a difficult craft writing is, and what a long road lies ahead of me to become a halfway acceptable writer." I don't believe that she felt secretive about the personal material in the narrative. Her general inclination was to share, especially where sharing could help others to lead better lives.

Our conversations about what we thought of as life's deeper meanings inevitably included the Holocaust. What she had to say on this subject didn't tell me much that I hadn't heard elsewhere, but it was reassuring to hear conflicting views weighed by someone of such discernment and to be dialoguing about these horrors with a fine human being who had emerged from pre-war Germany.

Having followed the family's fortunes to their arrival in the US, Renata devotes four single-spaced pages of *Detours and By-ways* in response to a question posed "not long ago by a young friend, an Australian Jew who has given much thought to his Jewish origins." Even now, in 1985, she writes, it is too early to see the "entire picture of the Holocaust," if indeed that will ever be possible. She wonders whether the Holocaust was different in kind and motivation from earlier pogroms and genocides and is inclined to think that it was not; that modern technology allied to the German "genius for organization," enabled an event different in scale rather than kind from earlier cataclysms. Recalling the conditions after the Treaty of Versailles in

1919 (like many German children she developed rickets, and was sent to Rotterdam to recover), she can to some extent understand how Germans who felt "victimized" could see in Hitler, "the embodiment of mediocrity," a savior. On the extent of collective guilt she writes: "Most Germans claimed, after the war, that they had not known the full extent of the atrocities. I used to dismiss that as blatant lies. I am not so sure anymore."

She used to talk often about how "sadists" were able to shape events and place their kind in positions of power over Jews and others, but she thinks that "quite ordinary" and decent people would have been caught up fairly innocently in the flow of events, perhaps turning a blind eye or not fully understanding. She writes also of those who resisted the madness—including local shopkeepers and residents who offered to protect her family, its non-Jewish name, Elsberg, already offering some protection—at their own grave risk. She concludes: "One thing is becoming more and more clear to me: fanaticism in any form is the greatest threat in our age." Beneath it all, though, and running through our many conversations, was the sense that the human being is a doomed creature—gifted but catastrophically conflicted – whose brilliant cultural achievements mask a darkness that will ultimately prevail.

From perhaps the 1980s onwards we would talk by letter, and on the sofa when I visited, a lot about old age. Needless to say, Renata, a devotee of "the examined life," reflected upon it as it approached and as she moved through it. Old age, she writes in a letter of 1996, "is as many-faceted as adolescence and equally unpredictable." One memorable exchange occurred not on the sofa but in her car on the way to do some shopping. She observed, as she often did, that old age was interesting and even something of a relief in that you learnt to "live without a future." You woke up without any but the most practical short-term agendas and took each day as it came in a spirit of becalmed appreciation. Flashing one of her sober but playful smiles at me, she added: "And it's a relief not to be living through your genitals." When Mark and Jeff talked her into getting the internet, the octogenarian wrote to me:

> Esteemed Professor Freudman,
>
> Now that I have the internet I am receiving daily offers of penile enlargement. I am very tempted but I am seeking your learned advice before going ahead.

She was fascinated by the way the raw "compulsive" energies of earlier life give over to more reflective ones, and how reflection profits from a "diminishing emotional response," a less mercurial engagement with the world, as the decades pass. If occasionally lamenting her loss of acumen—she writes of her "gray cells" beginning "to leave for greener pastures"—by far her greatest regret is the loss of friends: the year before her death she writes, "How many more friends will I have to accompany to their final exits before I can leave?" She liked the spiritedness of Dylan Thomas –

> Do not go gentle into that good night,
> Old age should burn and rave at close of day;
> Rage, rage against the dying of the light.

– but distrusted the poem's refusal of acceptance. She detested the thought of becoming an old bore, "a pathetic old woman." One of the things that made her a marvelous mentor-friend was that she did not imagine that old age conferred final wisdom, nor complete disconnection from earlier failings and failures:

> (How easy it is to look back from the vantage point of old age and act "wise." I was quite stupid for a good part of my life!) … I still consider myself a work in progress and will continue to be one until the final hour.

As she moved deeper into her eighties she'd sometimes sign her letters "Your very old friend"—meaning both that we had been friends for a very long time and that she was indeed now "very old." During her final decade her mentoring focused a good deal on old age itself. She didn't fear death but she did fear illness that might incapacitate her and make her a drain on the family. She was determined to go quickly once the time came and was quite prepared for it to come soon. If I'd comment on my fear of death, or on how poorly the driven state in which I lived would prepare me for death, she'd reply: "If this is your state at this stage in life, you have to follow it. Change will announce itself, without a conscious effort on your part."

She remained remarkably active, writing regularly for the local community newspaper, the *Oyster Bay Enterprise-Pilot*, working on short personal narratives, corresponding with her wide circle of friends, doing her daily yoga and swims (she was the oldest participant to complete the

Nassau County Chapter's Annual Swim-A-Cross, the final time just months before her death). She remained devoted to her family, spending lots of time with her grandchildren, Andrea and Max, writing narratives to and for them. As Mark wrote in his eulogy, "She was there to talk to, to seek advice from, to listen, to love." When Margaretha was diagnosed with bipolar disorder the sense of *déjà vu* must have been highly disturbing for Renata, but she did her best to disguise her anxiety during times of family difficulty and was delighted when Margaretha's condition responded to medications that weren't available to Maria, and thrilled that a Long Island-based innovative concert series entitled *Ridotto*, designed and orchestrated by Margaretha, continued the Maimone tradition of live classical performance on Long Island. That series, in which Mark also plays a major role, continues to this day, twenty years after its inception.

Joe died peacefully from heart failure on 16 October 2001, aged eighty-eight. Not long after this, Renata started going through drawers and cupboards, throwing out what would not be of any use after her death.

I greatly regret that when I last saw her, in 2002, I was embroiled in one of my gloomy tangles. Diane and I had just decided (or so we thought) to separate. I must have been depressing company as I unburdened myself on the sofa and during walks along the beach, and this time, for the first time, I sensed that Renata just didn't have the strength to listen, sympathize and advise without being sucked into the gloom. She was very fond of Diane, and no doubt her energies were ebbing with age; but I think I read in her dismayed eyes a feeling that the once-young friend whom she'd expected to rise above the tragic and wasteful human patterns she'd seen over many decades had, in the end, succumbed, got stuck in some self-thwarting "byway" without the wherewithal to move on. Or maybe I'm falsely attributing my feeling of the time to her. I'm not sure, but I don't recall her saying before, as she did on this occasion, "Well, I want the marriage to last but this time I don't have such a good feeling."

When she dropped me off at the train station and we said our goodbyes I got out of the car, looked at her and waved. She couldn't muster a smile, but rather tilted her head to one side and rolled her eyes back as if almost in resignation. She returned my wave with a desultory waft of the hand.

The sense that Renata of all people might have come to doubt me steeled me to put important things right. Diane and I didn't separate. And Renata and I kept writing to each other. Our last exchange was in December 2004.

On 14 April 2005 a tearful Mark rang to say that Renata had died the day before. She'd suffered an aortal aneurism but had refused surgery that would probably have prolonged her life, preferring to fade painlessly away over a period of hours. She farewelled Andrea and Max individually and then lay talking calmly with her sons until she lost consciousness.

Her large funeral, at the Bayville Town Hall on a hot summer day, included music recitals, and eulogies from friends, family and the local mayor. Mark read a short tribute from me. This chapter is a much-expanded version of the eulogy I would like to have delivered had I been there.

I set an alarm, got up at 3 a.m. Melbourne time, and sat in a chair thinking about Renata as the funeral unfolded twelve thousand miles away. Some of what flitted through my mind is recorded in these pages. But there were other snippets, disconnected but quintessential, as our fragment-memories of important people often are:

> Renata cupping her hands around a spider that someone was about to kill because it had ventured into the house, and carrying it outside to the safety of the garden.
>
> Renata, all patient encouragement, teaching Jeff's Vietnamese wife, Hung, to play the piano.
>
> Renata, pausing mid-sentence to listen, enthralled and delighted, to the delicacy of Mark's phrasing as he practiced his cello a couple of rooms away.
>
> Renata roaring with laughter as Jeff and Joe traded gags.
>
> Renata, so thrilled by her grandchildren that in their company she seemed to see a world as shining and free of complication as theirs.

Seven months later, Jeff spread Renata's ashes, as she had instructed, at Stehli Beach, scene of their many swims together. Mark, knowing what the beach had meant to the two of them, left the occasion to Jeff who recorded it in a moving short piece called "The Last Swim."

> It was a cool, crisp November evening. I drove

the five minutes from home to the beach. Mom's ashes, on the seat beside me, were sealed in a plastic pouch inside a sturdy cardboard crematorium box. I was talking to "her," saying things like "I can't believe this is our last swim," and "This is really traumatic for me." Tears were running down my face. I tried to buck myself up.

The beach was completely deserted under a starry sky. I took the pouch out of the box and poked four small holes in the bottom to represent the four of us in the family. I went to where Mom and I used to enter the water, walked to the rock jetty by the creek club, and started to slowly shake the bag. The breeze picked the ashes up and they spread out in all directions and then settled on the surface of the water. Childhood memories of me and Mom at the beach came flooding back. On the way back I sprinkled the remaining ashes where the flags demarcate the swimming area in summer.

At the back of the parking lot is an old broken-down bathhouse with a shower on the outside. It's boarded-up and in ruins now because no one wants to touch it on account of the asbestos it contains, but it was in full operation when I was a child in the 1950s and 1960s. Not wanting to throw the box and the pouch into a trash can, I set them down behind the bathhouse, got back in the car and drove home.

In recent months Jeff has sent me many photos and

documents from Renata's life. I find the photos, which carry her all the way from her mother's arms as a tiny baby to the very late one that adorned the funeral invitation, extraordinarily poignant. I can only know this long and special life in snatches, joining dots that even her wonderfully frank reflections and conversations did not connect. I hope I have done it justice, have helped to leave a "copy" of this woman's "many graces."

How many truly wise people do you meet along the journey? When in Proust's *Guermantes Way* Marcel's beloved grandmother falls ill he refers to her as "She, in whose heart I always placed myself in order to form an opinion of the most insignificant person." Renata was fine, warm, loyal and truly wise. Even now, at sixty-four, my own old age opaquely imminent, if something puzzles, moves or distresses me, I find myself wondering: What would Renata have said?

Ten

The coming of age at Peconic

… entering upon that dim, murky period when regrets come to resemble hopes, and hopes are beginning to resemble regrets, and youth is fled, and old age is fast approaching.

—Ivan Turgenev, *Fathers and Sons*

———

Congressman Anthony Weiner, it seemed, had been texting photos of his briefs-enshrined congressional member to ladies who were not his wife. The gloriously appelled CNN anchor Wolf Blitzer and his panel of esteemed commentators, while acknowledging the folly of such intimate self-chronicling in the internet age, opined that, nevertheless, American *mea culpa* and time would see the young congressman rise again.

It was all a bit of a blur to me, slid in a chair in a passenger lounge at LA Airport, fourteen hours into the trip, another seven to kill before the six-hour flight to New York where we were to celebrate my sixtieth birthday with friends in an old house on a bay in Long Island.

I no longer relished travel: the thirty-hour hauls from Australia, the disruption of carefully choreographed domestic and work routines fashioned over the years to keep the Black Dog at bay.

It was a vast relief when Mark Maimone met us at Kennedy Airport. We stayed three days with him and Margaretha, near Huntington, Long Island, birthplace of Walt Whitman (leaves of paint now drift from the concrete walls of the Walt Whitman Mall) before moving an hour on to Peconic, near the tip of the island's North Fork. In the boot of the rental car was a set of Joe Maimone's old golf clubs.

I never quite feel that I've checked-in, come to rest. There is always a pull, an undercurrent, wanting to tug me out of the moment, toward a more perfect, imagined future. Michel de Montaigne says that "no one is arrived at himself," and I guess this is true, though more for some than others. For Jay Gatsby it was not an undercurrent but a green light across the water, a vision of an ever-elusive "orgastic future that year by year recedes before us. It eluded us then, but that's no matter—to-morrow we will run faster, stretch out our arms farther." And for me, as each new future shimmers into view, dumb optimism's inner voice says "*That* will be the place. Make it *there* and all will be well."

I half-believed this as our car threaded its way through Peconic woods, then rounded a long curved driveway ending beside a rustic timber shed. We made our way along a cobbled path to the front lawn and gazed in wonderment.

A beautifully proportioned Dutch Colonial house

stood serenely in a sweeping sculpted garden, its gabled roof overarching shingled walls with dormer and white-shuttered windows. Steps led up to a white wooden portico supported by plain white columns, American flags aflutter, and thence to a rough-hewn white door. The main body of the house rose majestically to three storys, the roof of the lower section repeating the line of the one above, and seeming to gently anchor the great structure in its generous but intimate surroundings.

We followed the lush lawn around the left side of the house and there below, serene, still-blue-gray in the summer sun, were Hog Neck Bay and Little Peconic Bay, the South Fork of Long Island just visible on the horizon. Steep stairs led down to a private beach. Turning to survey the back of the house we were surprised to find that its rear door and entranceway were almost as ample and welcoming as those at the front. The house seemed to face two ways—out from its commanding position on the bluff and over the bays, and in toward the garden where the curving lawn traced beautifully maintained beds of modest bushes, shrubbery, blooming roses, and then gradated into wild grass and woodland. A dead gray blasted tree, inclining at forty-five degrees as if caught in an eternal Dantean wind, conducted the eye to a small pond girdled by ornate wrought iron.

After taking it in for a time we found the keys hidden as per our emailed instructions, and let ourselves in. Passing through a modern kitchen we came to the entrance hall with its aged oaken floorboards, white plaster walls, hand-cut lacquered beams and soaring stairway to the two floors above. We knew from the internet advertisement that the house was in some way connected with an artists' colony, but we were astonished to find ourselves in a virtual gallery, the walls lined with original artworks—traditional portraits, landscapes, still lives, narrative paintings of mythological scenes, sketches, and modern semi-abstract seascapes.

In the advertisement the current owner explained that the house:

> has been a special place for my family for four generations. It was begun by my great-grandparents, who moved the house to its beautiful location in 1911 to be part of an artists' colony. As a child I enjoyed every summer here with my grandparents and now return often with my husband and children.

How, I wondered, could anyone have moved a vast structure like this? And what sort of artists' colony would have known such grandeur?

Bedrooms on the second and third floors had views of the garden and the water. We unpacked and waited for our friend, Rick Shapiro, and his family, to arrive. Diane took to a hammock with a book; fifteen-year-old Elliot made acquaintance with the cable TV in the living room; I took Joe's 9-iron into the garden and chipped a couple of balls around the tranquil grounds.

My friendship with Rick Shapiro dates back to undergraduate days at Brandeis University, and has been warm and enduring over almost forty years. As his car rounded the drive, my spirits soared. For me, renewing friendships is the finest thing about travel. A rotund but fit almost-sixty, with a square head and intense brown eyes, Rick's vertebrae-cracking hug and high-pitched welcoming laugh were about as good as it gets. There's a marvelous life force about this penetratingly bright, sometimes obsessive, always loyal man. Rick lives with high seriousness but, unlike me, retains the capacity for cloudless pleasure in the moment and doesn't get down unless something serious is wrong.

With him was his wife, Penny, a professional violinist, their twelve-year-old son, Ben, and Penny's eighty-nine-year-old mother, Joan, who had left the UK to live with them near Boston a few years back. Rick's son by his first marriage, Adam, would take time off his Wall Street job to visit later; our daughter, Madeleine, then twenty-three, and brother, Ben, thirty-three, would arrive in a few days from Australia after university exams. We'd defer my birthday meal until then.

We all walked, delighted, through the great old house and then the adults congregated, beers in hand, on the front lawn. Rick and I Skyped often but this was the first time we'd been together in six years. We were toasting our good planning and our good luck when a navy blue Ford juddered to a halt beside Rick's car. A woman, perhaps in her sixties, flung herself from the driver's seat, waved frenetically and strode toward us.

She had shortish gray, rather unruly hair. The bright orange of her large plastic-framed sunglasses was repeated in her sandals and in the flaming floral design of her loose-fitting summer skirt. As she drew closer I saw a weathered but impassioned face probably older than its years.

"You must be the Shapiros and friends! Wendy has told me all about you! Welcome to High House! I'm Prue, a friend of the family. They asked me to show you round."

"Well, it's just a pleasure to be here. This place is Edenic," I said.

Some incidental chatter, and then, suddenly, her gaiety dissolved. "You know about the ticks, don't you?"

"Well," said Rick, "ticks are common in these parts. Nothing to worry unduly about."

"Oh, my goodness!" she said. "You *must* worry, you *absolutely must!*"

Now began a near-death narrative to sap the spirit of even the most sanguine holidaymaker. The woods, it seemed, were teaming with deer and the deer were teeming with ticks. She herself contracted Lyme's Disease from one of these sinister parasites and it almost killed her.

"My joints were agony. *Agony!* I felt a hundred-and-twenty. I was so sick I wanted to die. I couldn't move. Couldn't do anything. My life was in ruins. One day driving into Manhattan to see a specialist my arms were so painful"—here she extended both arms like a blind woman bereft of her cane—"that the tears were streaming down my cheeks. I could hardly see!"

We agreed that this was a horrendous state of affairs. My hypochondriacal tendencies aroused, I asked whether there was any way of warding off such bug-borne calamity. Rick mentioned an effective repellent that was readily available.

"Yes," conceded our Orange Cassandra, "but you must cover yourself in it every time you go outside. They're not just in the long grass and the bushes—the lawn is alive with them!"

Have I just been playing Kamikaze golf? I wondered.

Rick tried to deflect the conversation, but there was no stopping her.

"You must check for them under your arms," she advised, raising each arm and inspecting her armpits like a chimp in a family grooming session. "And also *here*," she instructed, vigorously rubbing her groin. "Always check your private parts!"

Diane listened in forbearing astonishment. I could sense that Rick's patience was ebbing but there were practical questions he wanted to ask about the house and the area.

By now I was, as it were, ticked-off. *I didn't need this! What did this woman think she was doing, welcoming people who had flown halfway round the world to rent this lovely house with tales of catatonic infestation?!*

I dropped one of the golf balls into the grass and began chipping my way toward the safety of the back lawn, checking my calves every few paces for pea-sized short-legged black assassins, leaving the others to the Tick Lady's apocalyptic ministrations.

The house was configured for perfect accord between solitude and sociability. The men, all too predictably, set up work stations—Rick, an independent Shakespeare scholar and businessman, by the front door, me by a first-floor window at the back of the house looking out over the water. Elliot and Ben took possession of the technology-enhanced, antique-furnished, painting-lined living-cum-dining room. The wives, each a voracious reader and each needing a break from demanding work lives, settled into more peripatetic routines, drifting between house and garden, hammock and outdoor leisure chairs, beach and garden. Rick, who was a fine cook, also frequented the kitchen.

I don't know about him, but my set-up by the window, at an antique desk with a rickety chair, was more a matter of having intermittent access to protective rhythms, long-established to keep the Black Dog on its leash, than it was about doing work, though I did pick away at various things. Even here, in this superb place, among family and friends gathered to celebrate my sixtieth birthday, hungry old empty feelings sometimes broke the surface of our twinkling calm, as if demanding a seat at the birthday feast.

It was laughable to think of the great house as a "holiday rental," a place of fleeting convenience for beach-going tourists. It was a living piece of a lovely past, effortlessly accommodating modernity's techno-gadgets and comforts without sacrificing its own sculpted leisurely rhythms. It exuded story—from the faint resin scent of lacquers, the creak of floorboards, the framed mythic scenes, the portraits of unknown folk who may well have lived or dined here. It was superbly welcoming, as if simply pleased to see you enjoying your short stay; yet there were times when for me its history beckoned more than the bays below, more even than the family fun we'd come for—swimming, bike riding, sport, touring the local vineyards. But of course a kid playing Xbox cares not whether the chair he sits in is three hundred years or three months old.

And so I resolved only to dip briefly into the books—some old, others straight from airport stands—that lined the dark-stained shelves above and behind the desk. Whitman was a natural for this collection, which contained a good sampling of classic American literature. *The Great Gatsby* was a natural too. After all, this was Gatsby country, and as I leafed through the old hardback edition of F. Scott Fitzgerald's classic I imagined gazing out of that window toward the South Fork and seeing something like the green light that drew that gauche, self-immolating, luxuriant Long Island dreamer, Gatsby, on. Could two more different great houses be imagined—this one and Gatsby's mansion?

Perhaps I should have stopped there, but further browsing brought me to a tall book on a lower shelf—*Painters of Peconic: Edith & Henry Prellwitz*. Since the current owner was named Prellwitz, perhaps this book, with its glossy hard cover featuring what looked like an Impressionist image of the bays the house looked out over, would explain who these artists and their "colony" were and even disambiguate that strange advertisement snippet—that the house itself had been "moved" to its "current location." The book was the catalogue of an exhibition held in September 2002. It contained essays by two scholars whom I later learned were eminent students of New York art: Ronald G. Pisano and William H. Gerdts. The first, by Pisano, featured short biographies of Edith and Henry Prellwitz. At first glance it seemed also to tell the story of their magnificent house. I flicked quickly through it, set it down on the desk and joined the families for lunch.

Late that afternoon I returned to the desk and read the first chapter. Here, in summary, is what it revealed:

Around the spring of 1892 an up-and-coming young American painter, Henry Prellwitz, hired a studio in the Holbein Building, 152 West Fifty-Fifth Street, New York. A year or so earlier, another fine young painter, Edith Mitchell, had taken a studio directly across the hall. The two had known each other for some years, first as students at the Art Students League of New York and then as art students in Paris. During the Holbein Building days a deeper bond formed and the two, by now significant young figures in New York art, married on 6 October 1894. They lived (with their son, Edwin, who was born in 1896) in New York City for the next seventeen or so years, often vacationing at a summer house in Cornish, New Hampshire, where they enjoyed the company of a colony of painters, artists and musicians.

In 1899 the Prellwitzes rented a house in Peconic, a rustic but cultured, wooded area, popular among artists, within easy distance of Manhattan. While not perhaps rich, the Prellwitzes were of comfortable independent means.

They planned to purchase this house and to maintain an apartment in Manhattan; but in the summer of 1911, on a drive in his recently acquired car, Henry was fascinated by a house that stood vacant and for sale in Aquebogue on the North Fork. Built around 1814 by Joshua Wells, a local identity, it was named High House Josh, because its three-story Dutch Colonial structure, copied in part from New York townhouses, made it the tallest in the area.

Henry fell in love with the place and Edith was equally thrilled when he took her to see it, but there was a catch: they'd purchased a block of land on the bluff at Peconic, thirty miles away, looking out over the bays, and had hoped to build there. What to do?

Now came the astonishing bit: at a time when such a thing was very seldom done, the Prellwitzes decided to move the house by sea.

High House Josh's grounds ran down to an inlet on Great Peconic Bay. Under the supervision of a local carpenter, the house was dismantled, the pieces carted to the inlet, loaded onto a scow towed by Henry's power boat, and reassembled on the bluff at Peconic. Ronald Pisano's account of this relocation feat is reasonably detailed, but it struck me as so extraordinary that I wanted to know more. We'd been told that a thesis had been written on the topic, so when we returned to Melbourne I wrote to Wendy Prellwitz, the current owner and the artists' great-great-granddaughter, to inquire further. Wendy, it turned out, was a Boston-based architect and painter, many of whose tranquil semi-abstract seascapes hang in the house. Generously, she sent me an attachment containing what was her MA architecture thesis. This loving and lovely document contained the description I was after:

> First of all, each beam, casement, door, panel, and other various parts, was carefully numbered and indexed … Apparently the 30 mile trips became quite an occasion for Henry and his [artist] friends. When the scow got to the site, a clearing in the cedar and oak woods, it was beached. Horse-drawn wagons pulled the timber parts and bricks up the embankment. The foundation was laid with the original bricks, which were rather unusual. They were varied in colour and not a uniform size as bricks are today. At last, in 1912, under the supervision of George Horton, the house was raised.

The Great Gatsby is set in 1922, a mere ten years after High House assumed its stately but understated position on the bluff. In faded photos of the time, artists including the Prellwitzes, Edward August Bell, Irving Wiles and Charles Bittinger, pose in casual attire, or sit in earnest conversation in the great house. The Roaring Twenties is not just years, but light years away. To the right of the main house the Prellwitzes built two large studios under a single roof. To this day they contain many of the couple's original artworks and are still used by the family. Later, their son Edwin, a landscape architect, did most of the garden. One could hardly imagine "a place for which nature had done more, or where natural beauty had been so little counteracted by an awkward taste." Relocated and reassembled, High House Josh became just High House—its name in the internet advertisement Diane saw almost a century later.

⸺◦⸺

There was something quite wonderful about the way the fine old house, now in its fourth generation of the Prellwitz family, welcomed and accommodated the generations of holiday makers and their friends, fleeting cohabitants with other longer-term residents—those mostly anonymous folk whose portraits lined the walls. Above "my" desk was a superb oil portrait, as Wendy was later to explain, of Edwina, daughter of Edwin, granddaughter of Edith and Henry, painted by Edith in the manner of John Singer Sargent. Wendy also explained that another of Edith's portraits—of an aging, cheerful woman who looked with welcoming benignity down on the landing as I made my way to our bedroom or my desk—was a Parisian flower lady.

The least settled of the current occupants' rhythms belonged to Penny's mother. I'd first met Joan twelve years earlier at Rick and Penny's house in Wayland, Massachusetts, and had been much taken by the special aura she had: sensitive, nuanced, clear-headed, confident, but without the least trace of dogmatism; highly principled but also tolerant and inquiring. In her late seventies then, she moved with a litheness, an almost balletic deftness, that belied her years. I wasn't surprised to learn that she had been a promising dancer before the war set her on a lifelong path of caring for others.

Now on the cusp of ninety, short-parted white hair framing her gently receptive face, Joan was as likeable and admirable as ever. But life was becoming more difficult for her. Though still quite hale for her age, she walked with a cane and a slightly ponderous determination edged with caution. She was generally alert, responsive, and engaged, but often disconcerted to find that very recent things had a habit of slipping from her mind. Late on the first afternoon, she turned up apologetically on the arm of a policeman, having taken a beach walk and forgotten the way back. Though she was delighted with High House and the gathering of family and friends, the grand old house became something of a torment for her. Often forgetting where she'd left her glasses, or a book, a hat, her handbag – worst of all, her cane—she'd wander disconsolately down corridors and up stairs, peeping into bedrooms, closets and darkened corners, asking ever so politely whether one might by any chance have seen this or that. Embarrassed and bemused, she'd feign amusement at herself, as if making clear to herself and us that she was sufficiently sound of mind to know when hers was playing tricks on her.

"Gosh I'm silly! I could have *sworn* that I left my glasses on the kitchen table, but I'll be *blowed* if I can see them! You haven't seen them by any chance, have you? So sorry to bother you. It really is a mystery! *Gosh*, I'm cross with myself!"

Even for this good-natured and accepting woman the frustration could become too much, and her tetchiness at times strained Penny's loving patience. These early visitations of dementia left great swathes of Joan's earlier memories intact. Indeed, recollections of her life from childhood through to the first stretches of old age remained acute and secure. But the recent past—say, what she had done in the foregoing weeks or days—was inclined to shift about in her mind. She was a talker and a sharer who spoke freely of her earlier life, but sometimes she would forget that she'd recounted this or that life experience already and could tell one person the same story, with little or no variation, twice in a day. It was becoming more difficult to align old and new memories and she was having to work hard to keep herself securely moored in the present. I think that despite the constant solicitude of her family this left her prone to a kind of loneliness. She was enormously grateful whenever someone listened attentively to her stories. So far as we were concerned it was a pleasure and a privilege to share them with her.

Perhaps two or three times she told me (and presumably others) the harrowing story of her son's death in his twenties: how the police had delivered the news; the shattering effects of a catastrophe that she, already a widow, and Penny, had to bear. She spoke of a period of absolute bleakness when she lived like an automaton; and then how, at a certain point, something changed: "I realized that I had to dig myself out of the pit. Life had to go on."

When we rose from the table after the first time she told me the story she leant forward, her cane still propped against the arm of her chair, and hugged me.

"It's so wonderful to have people to talk to."

It was hard for Penny, who had to watch the slow erosion of Joan's capacities and to negotiate that fine and hitherto independent woman's increasing dependence on her. She was managing all of this while parenting a boy on the cusp of adolescence, earning a living as a professional musician, and sharing all of this with Rick, a fine but compulsively busy man.

Diane also had a lot to contend with. No sooner had she flopped into the hammock with a book than a problem email would arrive from her cutthroat corporate workplace, despite her being on annual leave. Maddie would be arriving soon, and the long flight over was bound to upset her fragile mood cycles, and require a good deal of support. Diane had no elderly parent to worry about (her father had died three years earlier and her mother was in good health), but in me she had a complex life-companion, who had trouble being exuberantly "in the moment," even on an occasion like this. She'd gone to so much trouble over this holiday that she ought not need to be concerned about whether it was living up to my expectations. But I knew that she was concerned, and I understood why.

And so to this exquisite place we all brought many good things—good will, love of family, passionate interests and attachments, gratitude for what were flourishing lives – along with various complexities, some highly personal, others products of our postmodern cultural worlds. Unlike the kid in the antique chair at his Xbox, I was at times bemused by a feeling of cultural disparity between the style of the holiday we were having and our "holiday house." That feeling snapped into focus when in *Painters of Peconic* I read a comment that Henry Prellwitz made in 1927 about Modernism: "I am not ready for it yet ... I do not like Matisse or Cezanne." Matisse has long been my favorite painter.

No doubt being of independent means enabled the Prellwitzes to realize a mode of life unthinkable to the majority of their contemporaries. But Edith's diaries show this enviable life to have been scripted, chosen, shaped, quite as much as gifted by good fortune. She too had been complex, torn, ambitious, at least in her early adult life. Pisano quotes striking excerpts from a diary the young woman kept. At twenty, in 1883, shortly before commencing formal art studies, she writes:

> The teens have gone—what will the twenties bring? I am a woman of "aspiration," with ambitions and strong intentions to fulfill this ambition—to become an artist, a great artist. This is not a passing fancy and dream, but a steady purpose.

It was, in the very best sense, steely as well as "steady," since in choosing to put art above all else she was defying the gender scripts of her time. "The wretched devil Doubt has assailed me and worries me," she writes in 1885. "What if I am neglecting my home duties and following merely a vain ambition?" Later, in the same year: "My heart is dark and heavy ... Life is all a mistake. I am a mistake. I love nothing—I care for nothing on earth but art—and a few friends. I have but one aim and ambition and if that leaves me it will be despair." So powerful is her desire to be an artist that she fears that it overrides her love for her mother; indeed it represents for her a kind of marriage. Addressing her mother in her diary she writes: "Dear poor mama … a stronger tie is drawing me than holds me to you. I regard my work as sacred as marriage." Four years later, and nine years before she married Henry, she co-founded the Woman's Art Club of New York, later to become the National Association of Women Artists, in order to enact "the belief that serious consideration of the work of women could be won only when it could be shown in sufficient quantity to demonstrate that creative achievement need carry no sex discrimination."

She'd helped shape the world that Penny, Diane and Maddie had inherited.

———

Most of the artworks hung where the boys had established base camp in front of the TV/Xbox/DVD/CD systems. In order to peek at the mythic scenes, portraits, sea and landscapes, I had to pick my way through thick and often slippery ground cover—wet bathers, boxer shorts and towels, CD and DVD covers, basketballs, baseballs, footballs, thongs, track shoes, dead pizza boxes, potato crisp wrappings, scrunched Coke cans and bottles, books, notebooks for keeping score in games (especially Trivial Pursuit), dirty bowls and dishes, laptops, iPods, iPads, Game Boys, to name the deposits closest to the surface. Elliot, generally the most peaceable of people, took his customary perverse pleasure in bidding me to witness the sadistic mayhem of his Xbox games. Ben, readily taking his cue from the older boy, became likewise insistent. The exploding heads, Jurassic colossi, android assassins and the baleful apocalyptic background music were so remote from the artworks on the walls that I felt like an android myself, clomping simultaneously through three or four utterly separate realities. It was a relief when Elliot would occasionally pause the techno-mayhem and strum me a few riffs of Jimmy Hendrix on the acoustic guitar that came with the house. Hendrix was as close to my heart as to his.

And so I'd tiptoe through the refuse, straining to ignore the sound effects of carnage, *Painters of Peconic* in hand as I tried to identify some of the artworks on the walls and to understand what manner of artists these had been. I hoped too to understand more of the artists' colony and High House's place in all of that. A year later, I obtained the catalogue of the second exhibition, held in 1996 – "Henry and Edith Prellwitz and the Peconic Art Colony"—which helped to fill out further details.

The Prellwitzes became award-winning artists in their day; according to Pisano, and the two "made significant contributions to the cultural heritage of the United States." High House often held gatherings of a group of artists, including Bell and Wiles, and Benjamin Rutherford Fitz— which became known as The Peconic Art Colony. The two exhibitions that had become catalogue books revived their reputations after a fifty-year period of neglect following their deaths.

In the interview in which Henry records his resistance to Modernism, he qualifies his position thus: "I suppose most of my life I have really been influenced more by Thomas Dewing than anyone else. It has always been a struggle between that and the modern." Dewing, I was to learn, was a prominent American "Tonalist" painter—a style inflected by Pre-Raphaelite moods and themes, which frequently depicted the lightly draped female figure in moody, gray, shadowy landscapes. Tonalism was distinctly pre-modernist in intention and style. Hence the several paintings of mythic scenes featuring scantily clad female figures on the walls.

The less narrative landscapes adorning the boys' Pleasure Dome—images of the Peconic landscape, the bays, the house itself, paintings that Edith did of Manhattan skyscrapers—are strikingly reminiscent of European Impressionism; and Edith's portraits of Edwina and the Parisian flower lady are exquisitely painterly—their subtly vibrant, layered colors and relaxed lines an empathic contouring of the real with little *avant garde* transformative aspiration. An hour from Manhattan, the great house and its grounds and the artworks on its walls were easeful in part because they were pre-Modernist in sensibility (though Edith seems to have been less resistant to Modernism than her husband). Many of us, myself included, hanker for such ease, but even that great house could not simply confer tranquility like a spiritual dispensation, certainly not in two short weeks. My modern (postmodern?) self felt angular, almost arrhythmic, in this burnished haven from a bygone age.

I seemed to enjoy the garden most when I was chipping a golf ball around it. Apparently, I'm too highly strung to doze in the sun on a beach or in a field. The Tick Lady, however, had ruffled the surface of even this benign sporting pursuit, so that, despite the fact that only one tick was spotted (on Ben) during our entire two-week stay at High House, I would not take my stance beside a golf ball without having first taken militaristic protective measures: I'd don shoes and socks, track pants, no matter how hot the day, a long-sleeved white cricket shirt, a capacious floppy white hat, and enough specially formulated insect repellent on face, neck and wrists to keep an entire herd of deer parasite-free. The other lurking danger was said to be poison ivy in the wild grass and flowerbeds, though I was damned if I could tell this three-leafed menace from various harmless weeds that proliferated on the outskirts of the garden's sweet zone of domestication.

The Twin Threats—potential death by flora or fauna – concentrated the mind nicely: no wild swings, just controlled, measured short strokes, eyes on the ball, chips aimed at expanses of lawn well away from flowerbeds and—heaven forbid!—long grass or woods. If my life depended on it, could I always chip straight? Alas no: there were times when the ball would slew off the face of the club, or I'd over-hit in search of the perfectly rhythmical swing and the white orb would fly or bobble into a zone of imminent danger. My intense general dislike of waste and forfeiture means that I will go to any lengths to recover a lost golf ball. These patterns run so deep that not even the Twin Threats could defeat them. Those adjourning to the front porch with a cup of coffee or a beer might see me, swaddled in varieties of protective gear, lathered in cattle dip, arms fully extended, gingerly prodding, with golf club, rake or whatever I could find in the tool shed, at leaf mounds, grass tufts and dead branches that might be harboring an errant golf ball.

———

But I wasn't the only fool on this birthday errand.

Penny, formerly a violinist with the London Philharmonic Orchestra, was a perfectionist of positively philharmonic proportions. Having discovered a program that claimed to enhance neurological functioning via self-administered brain stimulation, she embarked in her orange top, green shorts and white sneakers upon peripatetic pilgrimages of self-improvement around the High House grounds, occult messages disclosing themselves to her through large padded headphones. Sometimes she'd stand under a tree from which she'd attached a tennis ball that bobbed on a string at head height. With the woozy pugnacity of a cuckolded rooster, she'd gently bunt the ball against her forehead, rhythmically thrusting her head forward for each new iteration.

———

My good friend Mark, an occasional visitor to High House, was a remarkably powerful golfer, childhood lessons having honed his swing well enough to ensure distance but alas not accuracy. On a lovely flat course nearby, the two of us armed with a set of Joe's clubs, he laid siege to the houses that lined the course, balls pinging off roofs, just missing windows, endangering life. Despite the course being flat and ideal, many of my shots—though straight—skimmed and bobbled, posing no threat either to houses or to the scorecard. In the car on the way home we blamed our age, recalling some of Joe's gags, like the one about the antique couple, he 102, she 101 years of age, who tell their lawyer they want a divorce.

"But why *now?*" the flabbergasted lawyer asks.

"We were waiting for the kids to die."

———

At a certain point, I turned sixty, though in this situation a fact so apparently settled as one's time and date of birth became something of a puzzle. The fact is that I turned sixty in Melbourne fifteen hours before I crossed the threshold in Peconic. I dwelled for fifteen hours in a curious liminal zone, unsure whether to attribute my lack of inner repose at the time to late-middle or early-old age. Such conundrums were delightfully compounded by the fact that, in a sense, the entire holiday was designed to mark and celebrate my birthday. It became a running gag that any piece of toast, cup of tea, or glass of wine was a way of marking my sixtieth.

Eventually Maddie arrived, badly knocked about by the flight, but not completely flattened, and then Ben; and so, three days after the day itself (give or take fifteen hours), we celebrated my birthday over lunch at a long iron table in gentle shade in the garden, on a glorious summer day, looking out over the bays. This was really something—all the kids now gathered, Rick and family, and Mark and Margaretha as well. We ate magnificently, drank white wine, beer and lemonade, talked and soaked in the view. If memory serves, I made one of my less pontifical and extended speeches, happy to float on an alcoholic haze until life as we know it reasserted itself.

⸺ ∞ ⸺

It was a moody place, up there in that book-lined space on the landing by the window. I don't think I felt particularly somber about arriving at a birthday that would have seemed antique to my younger self. Old age, though almost imminent, seemed as much an abstraction now as sixty seemed at twenty-six. I felt enormous sympathy for Joan in her impeded state, but I did not, except in a spirit of impersonal hypothesis, allow myself to think—to *really* think, to *concede*—that one day quite soon "this could be me," "the conceit of this inconstant stay." An inner power of dissociation that often accompanies sympathy for the suffering of others was very much in attendance.

Throwing a frisbee with the kids on that lovely back lawn was another matter. Old, imperfectly recovered elbow and shoulder injuries creaked and stabbed their reminders as my steepling throws landed ludicrously short, and my tall well-muscled sons sent the thing skimming three feet off the ground between the farthest points that the landscape would allow. Then I *felt* I was old, and aging fast. But even *that* wasn't quite cause for somberness. I could laugh that off, tell myself that I could still do many

274

other things. What made me somber then, I think, was my inability—which the boys no doubt felt—to be simply and delightedly *there*, lost in the moment with them, just having fun. But that was nothing to do with crossing sixty. That had long been me.

I had regrets aplenty, but they too were often somewhat abstract. They pulsed and throbbed in black moods and bad moments, but they didn't dog me as they might someone who was consumed by regret; and in good moods they would recede, emanating little heat—and even a little light. Yes, I dreaded death, but that wasn't my main concern. What I did not want was to go on living so little in the moment. In Thoreau's words, I did not want to go on devoting so much time to "what was not life." I needed a different weighting of the "now" and retrospection, of living and writing about it. Not the old brew of hindsight and apprehension, which conduced to a liminal state in which, as Turgenev says, "regrets come to resemble hopes, and hopes are beginning to resemble regrets."

To live otherwise was a spiritual challenge. But to name it thus was perhaps part of the problem. Challenges need to be "met," a word that radiates resolution, a clenching of the will. That metaphor wouldn't do now. I'd lived determined, clenched, for six decades. What was needed now was a giving-over, an Augustinian letting-in of light. Gatsby, that finally pitiful captive to tinny cultural myth who believed that "the rock of the world was founded securely on a fairy's wing," was of no use here. He could gaze out at that green light across the water and find nothing of substance there, and nothing within.

Edith did not keep diaries during her life at High House; nor do there seem to be extant letters from her time there. Her paintings of the gardens and bays have a lovely settled tranquility, as does a subtle pastel-colored interior of the hallway leading to the rear entrance of the house. How far these are simply "in genre" and how far an expression of her inner life during those years I cannot speculate. Pisano does however quote a journal entry in which, six months after Henry's death in 1940, Edith recalled his funeral: "It was snowing gently … when they buried him … a light beautiful snow—and a bird near the grave broke into song. Everyone remembers it, not me alone. It was all as he would have liked it. Quiet and beautiful."

Edith died four years later, and the couple are buried in Peconic, close to their beautiful home.

The fact that generations had come and gone in the old house became a part of what it meant to me to turn sixty. Clichéd though it sounds, there was the hope that the coming of age might involve seeing one's life and its steadily approaching cessation as part of something infinitely and consolingly greater. There was also the impulse to box on, to "not go gentle," as Dylan Thomas famously put it.

This wasn't just Gatsby country. Walt Whitman had been here too, a devotee of Peconic Bay and its environs. He often wrote in luminous appreciation of the coming of age. His "Youth, Day, Old Age and Night" invests old age with the inquiring dynamism of youth, the darkness of death with magical light:

Youth, large, lusty, loving—youth full of grace, force,
    fascination,
Do you know that Old Age may come after you with
    equal grace, force, fascination?
Day full-blown and splendid—day of the immense
    sun, action, ambition, laughter,
The Night follows close with millions of suns, and
    sleep and restoring darkness.

"Old Age's Lambent Peaks," a loosely autobiographical
poem that is also a paean to the accumulating wisdom of
autobiographical consciousness, is suffused with light of
various kinds and intensities:

The touch of flame—the illuminating fire—the
    loftiest look at last,
O'er city, passion, sea—o'er prairie, mountain,
    wood—the earth itself;
The airy, different, changing hues of all, in failing
    twilight,
Objects and groups, bearings, faces, reminiscences;
The calmer sight—the golden setting, clear and
    broad:
So much i' the atmosphere, the points of view, the
    situations whence we scan,
Bro't out by them alone—so much (perhaps the best)
    unreck'd before;
The lights indeed from them—old age's lambent
    peaks.

This was the lambent light that needed letting in, and
there were moods indeed in which I felt ready, even eager,
for the calm, clarifying retrospection of advancing years.

Whitman wrote "Youth, Day, Old Age and Night" at the age of sixty-two, eight years after he suffered the first of his "paralytic strokes." Remarkably, "Old Age's Lambent Peaks" was written in September 1888, at the age of sixty-nine, just three months after he suffered a second and very serious stroke. Two months prior to that crisis, however, he had penned a short poem about old age in a rather different mood and key. "Queries to My Seventieth Year," is an anguished, questioning cry, raw with the uncertainties of later life, the Bard's song-proclaiming voice now the harping screech of a parrot:

> Approaching, nearing, curious,
> Thou dim, uncertain spectre—bringest thou life or
>   death?
> Strength, weakness, blindness, more paralysis and
>   heavier?
> Or placid skies and sun? Wilt stir the waters yet?
> Or haply cut me short for good? Or leave me here as
>   now,
> Dull, parrot-like and old, with crack'd voice harping,
>   screeching?

A couple of days later Joan turned ninety. By now Adam had arrived, and Rick's parents, Marvin and Charlotte, had driven in from their retirement compound in Connecticut.

The big antique table in the living room, encircled by antique chairs and assorted ring-ins needed to seat us all, was elaborately set, candles flickering by each lace place mat, linen napkins in cloudy old silver rings. Red wine for the adults, Coke for the kids. Glasses ranged from exquisite crystal to blunt glass tumblers. The kids—dying to taste adulthood but not yet ready to forego Coke's kiddie world – got glasses for both. Carafes of water for those who'd lost the taste or the health for wine, or wanted to moderate its unwanted effects.

We'd been seated for a few minutes when Penny arrived with the guest of honor on her arm. Joan, slightly abashed at all the attention, was helped to her seat. The lights were turned off. Penny left for a moment and then reappeared, a gypsy "Happy Birthday" leaping from her violin. The meal, a collective creation of many hours, came in waves—cool, thin, spicy soup, seafood cocktails, roasted meat and vegetables. The burnished light threw translucent shapes upon the plaster walls, an old piano near the table, on the faces of the generations; the sound: chatter, snatches of earnest conversation, gags, anecdotes, bits of autobiography exchanged between those who didn't know each other well.

The table was cleared and a cake, adorned with candles that numbered many fewer than ninety, arrived. We sang the song with a gusto I hadn't heard since childhood and toasted Joan like royalty. Her ninety-year-old lungs huffed and puffed at the candles to surprisingly good effect, Ben only too happy to douse the remaining few with huge twelve-year-old exhalations.

And it was to young Ben that the honor of the first speech fell. Rising from his chair, his blue eyes flashing, the fringe of his dark-brown pudding-bowl haircut flying in the candlelight, he spoke of how much his grandmother had given him and his family.

"Every *hour*, every *day*, every *month*, every *year* she gives so much to me and my family. She has done *so much* for us, for *me!*"

He was flying now, fists punching out points like a politician as he soared to new heights, new points, and swooped to repeat ones already emblazoned upon the minds of his astonished audience. So towering now was his grand and impassioned eloquence that I wondered how he'd find the wherewithal to bring his great oration to a close. Rick was clearly wondering the same thing; wrapping a warm and proud fatherly arm around the boy, he said, "Okay, Ben, you've done great. You've made a great speech. Well done, Ben. It's time for Joan to speak."

Joan was by no means sure that she could or should manage a speech—"Goodness, I don't know what I can say"—but she knew she must and that indeed she wanted to; and so, with cautious care she rose to her feet, shakily setting her napkin to one side.

"This is *so* wonderful I hardly know what to say. To be here with my family and with so many wonderful friends. It's just *wonderful!* I can hardly believe it. It's *so nice* of you all to go to all this trouble. And thank you, Ben, for your lovely speech. And thank you all for cooking this wonderful meal. I can hardly believe my luck to be in this lovely place with family and friends. It's just so wonderful. I think this is the best birthday I've ever had. Thank you all so very

very much. Ninety years. I can hardly believe it. It's just wonderful. Thank you all again."

I felt my throat thicken, saw the flames dance and fuse into a pool of light, glow on moved faces, young and old, flit gay shadows across the portraits on the wall. I winked thanks to Diane for all she'd done to make this happen, and hoped that Joan could still look forward to a future rich in memories.

I'd have traveled thrice around the globe for this moment, and the old house, soon to celebrate its hundredth anniversary on the bluff in Peconic, seemed to heave a great satisfied sigh into the night.

Eleven
Fleur

And Death once dead, there's no more dying
then.

—Shakespeare, Sonnet 146

And so I retired and soon after that my mother, Fleur, died after a rapid deterioration in her health. Like most of us, she'd been frightened of illness and death for much of her life. As David Copperfield says of himself and little Emily: "We made no more provision for growing older, than we did for growing younger." Now suddenly Fleur felt that enough was enough. Perhaps at the last frontier of life, she had achieved the Stoic's "contempt of death" in which Montaigne believed so deeply—"dying" being "the greatest work we have to do," the hardest work, the one requiring most maturity, wisdom and spiritual equanimity. But if one had lived well, as he understood the Good Life – living reflectively, moderately, calmly—then death when it approached would not be a terror and, having lived well, one could die a good death. In my sixty-fifth year I think a lot about this.

When I told her a few months earlier that I had decided to take an early retirement package she asked two questions: "Will you remain a professor, dear?" and, "But what will you do with your time?"

Part of the answer to her second question is this book, which is dedicated to her memory.

I was also pleased to discover that my hitherto rather academic and literary interest in life writing could offer something to people outside the academy. I trained with Eastern Palliative Care and became a volunteer in their Biography Program, which assists terminally ill people to write their life stories; I trained and did some lecturing with Alzheimer's Australia, and ran life writing groups for people with dementia, under the auspices of Baptcare, with

Paula Bain; and I began lecturing on cancer memoir and assisting individuals living in remission to write their illness stories. I've been moved to find that there exists a vast army of volunteers, in various walks of life, many of them retirees who simply want to make the world a bit better for others.

Steadily, if intermittently and not without some backsliding, the professional life started to recede. The stepladder now sits at the base of the biography shelves in the Man Cave. I would like to say that "Things past redress are now with me past care," but that would be a fib. Old academic wounds can still throb. My favorite critic, Samuel Johnson, said this of some "scholists," literary scholars of his day: "there is often found in commentaries a spontaneous strain of invective and contempt, more eager and venomous than is vented by the most furious controvertist in politicks against those whom he is hired to defame." Not much has changed, and nor did I always contribute with seemly moderation to the kerfuffle.

Some things are now "past care" because they are opaque to recollection, and thank goodness for that. I love those late pages in Proust in which characters whom the narrative has followed for decades are now too old or infirm to recall against whom they nursed fierce enmities, or what those enmities had been about.

⁓

Like many people, Fleur could absolutely "fly off" if certain bare nerves—especially around trust and feared loss – were hit. I believe that the somewhat unsettling person she

284

could become then did not communicate much with what I think of as her core self, and that she did not know how changeable and troubled she could sometimes be. But that core self was deeply good and kind, passionately committed to improving a world whose injustices and cruelties she found almost too painful to contemplate. She was genuinely warm and often hilarious.

I owe her much for many of the things I most cherish – books, the life of the mind, the arts, humor, friendship. She'd be hugely amused to know that this book's loopy explorations of lives and life-story telling includes a biography of a pet. She followed the emotional lives of our cats and dogs with grandmotherly solicitude and delight, and adored my children.

Short periods in recuperative care facilities convinced this independent-spirited and sometimes feisty woman that she wanted to stay in her own well-appointed and handsome apartment until the end. And so a retinue of helpers of various kinds came in and out, one staying the night if she was particularly unwell.

The apartment was a forty-minute drive across town in traffic and one morning when it was my turn to call on her I felt particularly apprehensive as I set out. (My brother, Andrew, was of course around, but I do not presume to tell his story.) I'd made my way via the old art deco lift with its folding wrought-iron door that slapped shut before departure, along the light, carpeted painting-lined corridor to her apartment, through to the bedroom, and there she was, dead in her bed, looking serene and almost upright, as if she was about to comment on one of the books among a stack on her bedside table.

When the purpose-built black station wagon drew up that afternoon, two suitably solemn young men in *yarmulkes* made their way with a stretcher on wheels to the apartment. Some while later, when they were ready to remove Fleur from the building, I made my way down to the ground floor first so that I could meet them as the lift touched down. In due course the iron door clattered back and the two young men began gingerly to conduct my mother, now cocooned in a sort of zip-up bag secured to the stretcher with straps, out of her beloved apartment block.

But perhaps that old lift had seen better days, because it had come to rest just below the level of the floor and as one of the young men was edging backward out of the handsome old conveyance the heel of his right shoe caught against the raised edge of the floor, sending him tumbling, the stretcher tilting forward, and Fleur sliding into the entrance hall.

When Fleur, who had a glorious sense of the absurd, laughed, as she often did, she would throw her head back and roar. You could not help fall about laughing with her. She could also be, as I have said, feisty. I have an image of her now in some better place, looking down at that mishap in the foyer. Her first impulse would be to upbraid the young man. "You *bloody fool!*"

Then she'd worry about the emotional impact of what she'd just seen on me.

Later, though, holding court over afternoon tea with some of her many old friends, she'd recount the story, head back, howling with laughter, tears running down her cheeks.

References

Nowadays many references to modern and/or well-known texts can be traced online. In most cases, simply copy the italicized quotation fragment below into Google and details will come up. Where they don't, and for those who prefer the standard ways of doing things, here is a full reference list.

One: Stepladder to hindsight

—sensitive without being enthusiastic: George Eliot, *Middlemarch* (Cambridge, Mass: Riverside Press, 1968), 206.

—They cannot scare me: Robert Frost, "Desert Places", http://www.americanpoems.com/poets/robertfrost/691

—the long spasm of his too-fixed attention: Henry James, "Flaubert", *Essays in London and Elsewhere*, (New York: Harper & Brothers, 1893), 149.

—the terrible stringency of human need: Eliot, *Middlemarch*, 351.

—taking the world as an udder to feed our supreme selves: Eliot, *Middlemarch*, 156.

—the key to all mythologies: Eliot, *Middlemarch*, 206.

—like hearing the grass grow and the squirrel's heartbeat: Eliot, *Middlemarch*, 144.

—well wadded: Eliot, *Middlemarch*, 144.

—radical concept of retirement: Atul Gawande, *Being Mortal: Medicine and What Matters in the End* (London: Profile Books, 2014), 21.

—I, who watch myself as narrowly as I can, and who have my eyes continually bent upon myself: Michel de Montaigne, "Apology for Raymond de Sebonde", *Essays of Michel de Montaigne* (Chicago: William Benton, 1952), 274. Montaigne quotes, unless otherwise indicated, are from this edition. References will give essay titles for tracing quotes in modern editions, followed by Benton page numbers.

—Since God gives us leisure: Montaigne, "Of Solitude", *Essays*, 109.

—which is the greatest work we have to do: Montaigne, "Use Makes Perfect", *Essays*, 176.

—contempt of death: Montaigne, "That to Study Philosophy is to Learn to Die", *Essays*, 28.

—I have not the knack of nourishing quarrels and debates within my own bosom: Montaigne, "Of Cruelty", *Essays*, 203.

—I do not value myself on any other account than because I know my own value: Montaigne, "Of Presumption", *Essays*, 308.

—self-sufficient wellbeing: Marcel Proust, *Cities of the Plain*, vol. 2, *Remembrance of Things Past*, trans. C.K. Scott-Moncrieff

and Terence Kilmartin (New York: Vintage, 1982), 867.

–I do not paint its being, I paint its passage: Montaigne, "Of Repentance", *Essays*, 388.

–She was always trying to be what her husband wished, and never able to repose on his delight in what she was: Eliot, *Middlemarch*, 348.

–a man who could be interrupted with impunity: Henry James, *The Golden Bowl* (Middlesex: Penguin Books, 1966), 112.

–The description of the emotional sensation: Madeleine Freadman, "Description of bipolar mixed states" (unpublished 2013).

–alter the world a little: Eliot, *Middlemarch*, 107.

–the spray of phenomena: Samuel Beckett, *Molloy*, in *The Beckett Trilogy*, (London: Picador, 1979), 102.

–Our desires incessantly renew their youth: Montaigne, "All things have their season", *Essays*. Here I have used the Donald Frame 1956 translation, but the passage occurs in the Benton edition on 339.

–Some men are born mediocre: Joseph Heller, *Catch-22* (London: Jonathan Cape, 1962), 94.

Two: And what number do you wear, son?

–grimacing revenge: Tom Petsinis, *Four Quarters: A collection of poems* (Melbourne: Thompson Walker, 2006), 75.

Three: Cutting through

—Something there is that doesn't love a wall: Robert Frost, "Mending Wall", http://www.poetryfoundation.org/poem/173530

—nerves were brass or hammer'd steel: Shakespeare, Sonnet 120.

Four: The bigger you are, the harder they fall

—When I was a child, I spake as a child: 1 Corinthians 13:11, King James Version.

—that imagined "otherwise" that is our practical heaven: Eliot, *Middlemarch*, 343.

Five: The "logic" of life-changing "choices"

—the native hue of resolution: Shakespeare, *Hamlet*, *The Complete Works of William Shakespeare*, ed. W. J. Craig (London: Oxford University Press, 1962), 3.I.84. References are to act, scene, and line.

—By intellect and art I here have brought thee: Dante, *Purgatorio*, *Divine Comedy*, Canto 27.

—the Sea Hag was relaxing on a green couch: John Ashbery, "Farm Implements and Rutabagas in a Landscape", http://www.famouspoetsandpoems.com/poets/john_ashbery/poems/2687

—call spirits from the vasty deep: Shakespeare, *Henry IV*, part 1, 3.1.54.

—cocoon-like: Ian Guthridge, *Give Me a Child When He Is Young* ... (Melbourne: Medici, 1995), 1.

—To give full growth to that which still doth grow: Shakespeare, Sonnet 115.

—the bone-breaking burden of selfhood: Saul Bellow, *Herzog* (Greenwich, Connecticut: Fawcett Publications, 1965), 117.

—paving hell with energy: Charlotte Brontë, *Jane Eyre* (Middlesex: Penguin Books, 1966), 168.

—The lyric moves: Since I don't have verbatim recall of Grossman lectures, and since he wrote very much as he spoke, I have excerpted this passage from his study of poetry, *Summa Lyrica* in *The Sighted Singer: two works on poetry for readers and writers*, http://www.thedomesticbeast.com/write/an-excerpt-from-summa-lyrica-by-grossman

—principle of power invoked by all of us against our vanishing: Allen Grossman, http://www.allengrossman.com

—And sorry I could not travel both: Robert Frost, "The Road Not Taken" http://www.poetryfoundation.org/poem/173536

—And I am paralyzed: Allen Grossman, "The Recluse", *The Recluse and Other Poems* (Cambridge, Mass: Pym-Randall Press, 1965), 10.

—For / after a most careful search: Allen Grossman, "Meditation Three", http://allengrossman.com/poems/descartes.html

—while men's minds are wild: Shakespeare, *Hamlet*, 5.2.378.

—as way leads onto way: Robert Frost, "The Road Not Taken", http://www.poetryfoundation.org/poem/173536

—the general law of oblivion: Proust, *The Fugitive*, vol. 3, *Remembrance of Things Past*, 659.

−Popeye sits in thunder: Ashbery, "Farm Implements and Rutabagas in a Landscape".

−I had never lived: Guthridge, "*Give Me a Child*," 83.

−Ordination day was the unhappiest: Guthridge, "*Give Me a Child*," 112.

−my mind was like a sky fill with clouds: Guthridge, "*Give Me a Child*," 111.

Six: The challenged reader who mistook himself for a man of letters

−How is one to decide whether an inborn affliction: Arthur Koestler, *The Sleepwalkers* (London: Pelican Books, 1968), 240.

−−Lord have mercy upon me: Laurence Sterne, *The Life and Opinions of Tristram Shandy, Gentleman* (Boston: Houghton Mifflin Company, 1965), 359. Quotes from *Tristram Shandy* can also easily be traced on the Project Gutenberg text of the novel.

−The blood and spirits of Le Fever: Sterne, *Tristram Shandy*, 324.

−A COCK and a BULL: Sterne, *Tristram Shandy*, 496.

−Digressions, incontestably: Sterne, *Tristram Shandy*, 55.

−is digressive, and it is progressive too: Sterne, *Tristram Shandy*, 54.

−I hate set dissertations: Sterne, *Tristram Shandy*, 148.

–*old unhappy feeling*: Charles Dickens, *David Copperfield* (London: Chapman & Hall, 1890), 128.

–*Hobby-Horse*: Sterne, *Tristram Shandy*, 10.

–*on whose nature / nurture can never stick*: Shakespeare, *The Tempest*, 4.1.188–9.

–*O ye powers*: Sterne, *Tristram Shandy*: 153.

–*choose, between the things not worth mentioning*: Beckett, *Molloy, Trilogy*, 39.

–*the strange state of affairs*: Sterne, *Tristram Shandy*, 214.

–Tristram's plot diagrams: Sterne, *Tristram Shandy*, 359.

–*HOMUNCULUS*: Sterne, *Tristram Shandy*, 4.

–*a special kind of fatigue, or tiredness*: www.rch.org.au/kidsinfo/fact_sheets/Brain_injury_Cognitive_fatigue/

–*The anterior cingulate cortex starts to slow down*: My thanks to "Doc Bender" of the US Army whose account of this is the most succinct I've seen: www.dodlive.mil/index.php/2012/12/frontline-psych-with-doc-bender-why-cognitive-fatigue-matters/

–*A man like me cannot forget*: *Molloy, Trilogy*, 112.

–*reflects the misgivings of an ego*: Simon Lesser, *Fiction and the Unconscious* (New York: Vintage Books, 1962), 50.

–*When a story ensnares us*: Lesser, *Fiction and the Unconscious*, 192.

–*not spared by the mad need to speak*: Beckett, *The Unnameable, Trilogy*, 318.

—It is the nature of a hypothesis: Sterne, *Tristram Shandy*, 114.

—I shall never overtake myself—: Sterne, *Tristram Shandy*, 215.

—From their places masses move: Beckett, *Molloy, Trilogy*, 102.

—I invented it all: Beckett, *The Unnameable, Trilogy*, 228.

—I can't go on, I'll go on: Beckett, *The Unnameable, Trilogy*, 382.

—the bottom of the well: Sterne, *Tristram Shandy*, 193.

—DEATH himself knocked: Sterne, *Tristram Shandy*, 365.

—This then is the hinterland: Oliver Sacks, *Migraine* (London: Picador, 1992), 209.

—We envisage that psychosomatic reactions: Sacks, *Migraine*, 209.

—Case 75: Sacks, *Migraine*, 253–4.

—most motley emblem of my work!: Sterne, *Tristram Shandy*, 168.

Seven: Sauna talk

—I long / To hear the story of your life: Shakespeare, *The Tempest*, 5.1.311–13.

—All animals are equal: George Orwell, *Animal Farm* (Middlesex: Penguin Books, 1951), 114.

—death's counterfeit: Shakespeare, *Macbeth*, 2.3.83.

—For man is that ageless creature: Proust, *The Fugitive*, vol. 3, *Remembrance of Things Past*, 627.

—Proust's octopus: *The Guermantes Way*, vol. 2, *Remembrance of Things Past*, 308.

Eight: The black dog: Leo's life

—Psychoanalysts are missing important clues about their patients' childhoods: Kurt Vonnegut, *Palm Sunday* (New York: Delacorte Press, 1981), 146.

—*Argos passed into the darkness of death*: Homer, *The Odyssey*, bk 17.

—*the secret heroes of my vitality*: Mark Doty, *Dog Years: A Memoir* (New York: Harper Perennial, 2007), 14.

—*The attenuated nature … of individuality in animals*: Raimond Gaita, *The Philosopher's Dog* (Melbourne: Text Publishing, 2002), 77.

—*tell stories about animals:* Raimond Gaita, *The Philosopher's Dog*, 77.

—*I do not believe that the animals*: Raimond Gaita, *The Philosopher's Dog*, 20.

—*I'm quite sure she doesn't think anything*: Raimond Gaita, *The Philosopher's Dog*, 39.

—*More numerous than the hairs of my head are those who hate me*: Psalm 69, *The Tanakh: The Holy Scriptures* (Philadelphia: The Jewish Publication Society, 1985).

—*Dogs have been domesticated*: Goodall, quoted in Wolfgang M. Schleidt, Michael D. Shalter, "Co-evolution of Humans and Canids: An Alternative View of Dog Domestication: Homo

Homini Lupus?", http://www.academia.edu/3068541/Co-evolution_of_humans_and_canids, 59–60.

–hour of lead: Emily Dickinson, quoted in Doty, *Dog Years*, 142.

–It was only the trusting silent fellow: Doty, *Dog Years*, 143.

–A windy winter day: Doty, *Dog Years*, 17.

–go on with their doggy life: W. H. Auden, "Musée des Beaux Arts", http://www.english.emory.edu/classes/paintings&poems/auden.html

–one extended consciousness, reaching out in all directions: Doty, *Dog Years,* 91.

–Because dogs do not live as long as we do: Doty, *Dog Years*, 39.

Nine: Renata

–Shall you comprehend your mother, or only blame her: George Eliot, *Daniel Deronda* (London: Penguin Books, 1967), 692.

–a man to feel touched in the contemplation of: Dickens, *David Copperfield,* 629.

–very small village amidst green hills: Renata Maimone, *Detours and By-ways: Journey through a Life* (unpublished, 1985).

–the history of a liberation: quoted in Carolyn Heilbrun, *Writing a Woman's Life* (London: Women's Press, 1988), 44.

–more honour'd in the breach than the observance: Shakespeare, *Hamlet,* 1.4.16.

—you don't have to be a bad guy to depress somebody: J. D. Salinger, *The Catcher in the Rye* (London: Penguin Books, 1958), 152.

—too short for stretching out and the cover too narrow for curling up: Isaiah 28:20–21, *The Tanakh*.

—because it was he, because it was I: Montaigne, "Of Friendship", *Essays*, 85.

—Aristotle on friendship: *Nicomachean Ethics* (London: Penguin Books, 1955), 258–311.

—She, in whose heart: Proust, *The Guermantes Way*, vol. 2, *Remembrance of Things Past*, 323.

Ten: The coming of age at Peconic

—entering upon that dim, murky period: Ivan Turgenev, *Fathers and Sons* (London: J.M. Dent & Sons, 1938), 42.

—no one is arrived at himself: Montaigne, "Of Physiognomy", *Essays*, 507.

—orgastic future: F. Scott Fitzgerald, *The Great Gatsby* (Middlesex: Penguin Books, 1968), 188.

—a place for which nature had done more: Jane Austen, *Pride and Prejudice* (Middlesex: Penguin Books, 1972), 267.

—I am not ready for it yet: Ronald G. Pisano, *Painters of Peconic: Edith Prellwitz & Henry Prellwitz* (New York: Spanierman Gallery, 2002), 5.

—The teens have gone: Pisano, *Painters of the Peconic*, 8.

—The wretched devil Doubt: Pisano, *Painters of the Peconic*, 8–9.

—My heart is dark: Pisano, *Painters of the Peconic*, 10.

—Dear poor mama ... a stronger tie: Pisano, *Painters of the Peconic*, 10.

—the belief that serious consideration: Pisano, *Painters of the Peconic*, 12.

—made significant contributions: Pisano, *Painters of the Peconic*, 6.

—the conceit of this inconstant stay: Shakespeare, Sonnet 15.

—what was not life: Henry David Thoreau, *Walden* (New York: Holt, Rinehart and Winston, 1948), 74.

—the rock of the world was founded securely on a fairy's wing: Fitzgerald, *The Great Gatsby*, 106.

—It was snowing gently: Pisano, *Painters of the Peconic*, 29.

—Youth, large, lusty, loving: Walt Whitman, "Youth, Day, Old Age and Night", http://www.whitmanarchive.org/published/LG/1881/poems/96

—The touch of flame: Walt Whitman, "Old Age's Lambent Peaks", http://www.whitmanarchive.org/published/LG/1891/poems/365

—Approaching, nearing, curious: Walt Whitman, "Queries to My Seventieth Year" http://www.whitmanarchive.org/published/LG/1891/poems/315

Eleven: Fleur

–*And death once dead*: Shakespeare, Sonnet 146.

–*We made no more provision for growing older*: Dickens, *David Copperfield*, 57.

–*dying … the greatest work we have to do*: Montaigne, "Use Makes Perfect", *Essays*, 176.

–*Things past redress are now with me past care*: Shakespeare, *Richard II*, 2.3.170.

–*there is often found*: Samuel Johnson, "From Johnson's Preface to the First Edition", *Samuel Johnson: The Critical Heritage*, ed. James T. Boulton (London: Routledge, 2002), 158.

www.ingramcontent.com/pod-product-compliance
Lightning Source LLC
Chambersburg PA
CBHW070019100426
42740CB00013B/2561